Golf
God's
Way

Nove. 18, 2002

To
Thayne Wedde
Heartfelt Best Wishes for Not
only the best Golf but in your life!
Simplicity is the key word! Focus!
Focus! Focus!

Best Personal Regards
GusBernardoni

Golf God's Way

GUS BERNARDONI

Creation House • Carol Stream, Illinois

GOLF GOD'S WAY is published by BEI, 1067 Fair Oaks Ave., Deerfield, Illinois, 60015.

This book is manufactured in the United States of America.
Second edition
Originally published by Creation House.

Art and photography by David Swartwout
Design by Wendell Mathews

ISBN: 0-9629952-0-7
Library of Congress catalog number: 77-80414

Single copies of this book may be ordered by sending check or money order for $13.95 (includes postage and handling) to BEI at the above address.

*All honor and glory to God
through Jesus Christ
for miraculously delivering me
and allowing me to be a part
of this wonderful sport.*

*To my wife, Dorothy, and my family
who have sacrificed so much
in order for me to remain in golf
and to help others.*

*I wish also to thank Robert Walker
without whose help
this book would not have been written.*

Contents

FOREWORD

I'm a Christian. I'm also a golfer.

I firmly believe that every Christian golfer ought to read Gus Bernardoni's book. I also believe that every non-Christian golfer ought to read it.

Gus knows his golf—and he knows his God. A lot of folks don't realize that God is just as interested in the way we play golf as the way we earn our living and the way we spend any of our time. He says, in effect, "Whatever you do—do it well." And He offers to help!

This is what this book is all about: God's kindness in giving each of us special abilities with which to play the game. Gus Bernardoni tells us how to take advantage of them, and also he has some special advice for those with physical handicaps.

"Whatever your physical limitations may be—blindness, arthritis, a heart condition, back trouble, one arm, one leg—you can play the game of golf and enjoy it," says Gus.

Of course, God is also very interested in our priorities. Some people spend more time playing golf than they do thinking about God. That's a mistake, and that's why I think Gus's book is so valuable. Gus wants even the time on the golf course to be spiritually beneficial, as well as fulfilling for its own sake. And he offers great advice on ways to improve your golf game.

One of my most enjoyable times with God came about during a golf tournament in Nashville, Tennessee. It was the Annual Music City Golf Tournament, and I was paired with Chet Atkins and a couple of business "civilians" in that wonderful Celebrity-Amateur event that takes place each October in my own hometown. I was there for fun—but I liked the idea of winning, too.

It's a two-day event, and our foursome had done well enough the first day that we felt we had a fighting chance for the top trophy on Sunday. Though I asked for a late starting time so I could go to church first, it wasn't possible; our foursome had to tee off around 9:00 a.m. I felt a little uneasy about that, but Shirley, my wife, suggested, "Why don't you just worship God on the golf course?"

Now I don't in any way recommend spending Sunday on the golf course rather than in church, but I think this was a special situation. So, from the tee-off to the final putt, I was in constant dialog with the Lord, before, during and after every shot. Shirley strolled along with me that day, and my mother and dad joined us after church for the back nine.

We had an amazing round! I played one of the better games of my spotty career. Chet pointed his cigar in the direction of each hole, and seemed almost bionic in his precision. I think he played over his head that day, but so did our two business partners, as well. Each of us shot better than his handicap indicated that he should. And there were a couple of times when "miracles" occurred, like balls bouncing onto the green and into the cup, and exploding out of impossible situations in sand traps for little tap-in "gimmee" putts. Things like that.

All the way, I unashamedly (though folks usually laughed as if it were a joke) asked God to help me with my tee shot, my long iron shot, and an occasional long side-hill putt. The small gallery always chuckled, and I did a little raised-hand dance on the green when I sank an improbable par putt, usually with a stroke for a birdie. Mamma and Daddy thought we were crazy, and maybe just a little sacrilegious. But it was tremendous fun, and through all the chuckling and laughing, Shirley and I were serious.

And we won the tournament!

Ask some of the Christian pros on the tour right now: Rik Massengale, Tom Purtzer, Kermit Zarley, Gary Player, and some of the others. They'll tell you that you have to play well, really concentrate and do your best, but that it surely helps to know that God is interested in everything we do, even golf!

Each year, we welcome the Christian golfers' Bible study group to our home during the L.A. Open. There's always a sizeable group of 30 to 40 pros and their wives and friends. Either we provide a speaker or they just go ahead and conduct their usual Bible study. This year was special. Rik Massengale had just won the Bob Hope Classic, and Tom Purtzer was to win the L.A. Open that week. They, along with Gary Player and most of the golfers I mentioned, were at our home on Tuesday night, worshipping the Lord and sharing their experiences with Him.

I'll guarantee that those guys, when they settle over a $40,000 cut, are glad they have a "hot line to heaven." And they do!

Gus Bernardoni will tell you his story. It's a moving one and I do believe a rewarding one. He's learned a lot in his golfing career and in his relationship with God. He wants to share those lessons and discoveries with you and me. He makes golf seem simple, and it can be.

Enjoy it!   Pat Boone

Having known Gus Bernardoni since my High School days and having worked with him after his injury, I can well understand his interest and desire to help those with a physical handicap. I cannot imagine anyone better qualified to help them, as he knows well, the difficulties he encountered in his effort to succeed in golf, his chosen profession. This awareness puts him on a better common ground.

Indeed the principles written in this book should not only be used by the physically handicapped, but by anyone attempting to take up the game of golf. The ideas presented are simple and effective, putting the emphasis on the instrument placed in our hands (the golf club), and its use in order to propel the golf ball in a desired direction towards the chosen target.

The understanding of the golf swing must be simplified in order to make it simple to produce and repeat, otherwise, as many golfers have discovered, the game can be most frustrating. The ideas put forth here should permit the player to play golf with a better understanding of the golf club's motion - the swing.

I am certain that those who read this book will benefit from the views put forth by Gus Bernardoni, and that all will be inspired by his efforts to help others whether handicapped or not, and by his example to proceed to meet the challenges offered by the game of golf as well as those of the game of life.

Submitted by:

Manuel de la Torre, Head Professional
Milwaukee Country Club
Milwaukee, Wisconsin

The 17th (par 3) hole on the #3 course, Medinah Country Club in Medinah, Illinois. (Photo by Ed Feeney, Chicago Tribune; courtesy of John Marshall, Medinah Country Club).

14

The Hole That Got Away

INTRODUCTION

Saturday morning dawns bright and clear. What a day for golf! You reach the course, putt a few, step up to the tee and hit the ball straight down the fairway . . . long. You hit the second shot, a five iron, right on to the green. You putt the ball twice for a par.

The next five holes are a repetition of the first. Now you realize how Jack Nicklaus must feel when he is at work on the course—attacking and overcoming each hole.

Then disaster strikes. Your drive from the seventh tee is good. A six iron shot confronts you. You prepare as before, but this time you partially hit the ball which ends up in front of a trap to the right of the green. You walk to the ball and notice the flag is just beyond the trap. You take your pitching wedge and prepare more cautiously to hit the ball to the flag. Instead you hit the ball fat and wind up in the trap.

After you work your feet into the sand, mentally checking your points for a sand shot swing, you hit too

Disaster strikes

15

deeply into the sand. The ball moves only a few feet. Still in the sand you feel the tiny knot in your mid-section rising into your throat. Your face tells the story; you are going to get out or know the reason why. You grit your teeth, hold the club tighter . . . wham! The ball sails almost over the green. With blood vessels bulging on your neck, face slightly red, and jaw muscles set, you manage to hole out in two putts for a seven. Your friends don't help the situation any when they remark, "Back to normal, Herb?" Now, you are a candidate for bogey golf.

Candidate for bogey golf

"How can a guy blow like that?" you ask yourself.

Your Nicklaus feeling has disappeared completely. So what do you do?

Do you think for a moment that golfers who turn in sub-par scores have perfect form? Do they all have a picture-book swing? Not on your life! Their main concern is to get the ball into the hole. Is that your objective as well?

It is vitally important to use common sense in playing a shot; to use the club in a way that will achieve the desired end. This is a game of decision rather than mechanical excellence. A positive and aggressive attitude toward getting the ball to the green and into the hole is essential.

Objective: ball in hole

For instance, take the 17th (par 3) hole on the famed Medinah #3 course in Medinah, Ill. This is a long hole. The green is sloped steeply from back to front and somewhat from left to right. Traps guard the green on the left, left back, back, and front. A river runs in front of the green as well.

The wind from left to right coming down the river, with trees on both sides, swirls over the green increasing the difficulty of hitting the target.

If you hit the ball short, you land in the water or the trap in front. Hitting the front trap would not be bad, since you can blast up to the green. If you land in the trap left, you face a difficult shot. You must hit the ball above the hole to allow for the tremendous drift toward the water. When you hit the trap back of the green, you might as well change into your swimsuit.

So from the tee you look at a potential disaster. Muscle control alone will not make the shot a success. You choose the club you feel is best and hit the ball solidly without concern over the results. Though it is difficult to do, common sense can change your attitude from negative to positive. True, you can get into trouble on this hole, but you can also escape from traps and sink a long putt. You must think positively. Think
positively

On another course one day, my partner and I came to a par 3 hole with water in front of the green. He said experience showed he could reach the front portion of the water with a three iron, the center of the lake with a five wood, but could never get over the water and onto the green with his tee shot. He demonstrated his point.

"Since I can't get over the water, I hit short and then try to get as close to the cup as possible on my approach shot," he said.

It was my feeling he should reach the green easily with a five wood. With some coaching, he hit the ball well enough to clear the water. At my suggestion, he agreed to try an experiment. Using a six iron to hit short of the water, he plunked the ball into the lake—much further than he thought possible. So I suggested he use the five wood again and see what might happen. Sure enough, the ball sailed over the green and into the trap behind the green. Center on goal,
not on problem

"Why couldn't I reach the green before?" he asked in astonishment.

"Your mind was centered on the problem confronting you, not on the area into which you desired to hit the ball. You lost your ability to coordinate, to generate sufficient impact to send the ball that distance."

Many golfers have similar experiences. Why? Strong emotional impressions from past experience with the hole, the playing partner or opponent, the placement of the tee markers may focus the attention on the negative aspects of the game. The impact of fear, worry or doubt over a shot or score impresses one deeply.

However, it is possible to develop a positive mental attitude. Suggestions contrary to the successful outcome of the shot must be rejected. The golfer can attack each hole with fervent action of the club head, using common sense at every turn.

Attack hole fervently

When you exercise too much caution on any shot, any hole, any course, you have implanted the seed of negative response. After a shot has been made, avoid the "ifs": "if I had used another club . . . if I had made the dogleg . . . if I had cleared the trap . . . if I had made that three-footer . . . if I had four feet; four arms; two heads; Snead's action; Hogan's concentration; Nicklaus's distance."

Hit the ball with an aggressive, attacking attitude. This can be accomplished with a resilient, coordinated body. The hands must control the club at all times.

Use natural abilities

Use the natural abilities God gave you to the fullest.

The fiercest adversary, the most difficult and unmanageable problem, may be you!

True, life sometimes deals us a severe blow. Just as in golf, we often cannot seem to overcome, even though every conceivable effort has been made. In the spiritual life, many find that a talk with God through Jesus Christ is the first step in the right direction. So in golf. God is always waiting for you to turn to Him. There is a God-given method when all else has failed. You must prepare yourself mentally each time to attack the course and guard against adverse situations and people who disturb you.

All golfers face the same objective: to move the ball

from tee to green and into the hole in as few strokes as possible. That should be your only concern on the course. Be yourself; use your own coordination and instincts; hit the ball the best way you can. Each time you are confronted with a shot, proceed with singular purpose and concentration.

Golf God's Way

1

What has God to do with the game of golf? Actually, He has a great deal to do with your ability to play the game to the degree of perfection you desire. Moreover, He had much to do with the method of playing golf being introduced in this book.

You are a deliberate design of God. Your mental and physical qualities did not just happen. The mobility of your muscular system enables you to do all that you do. This includes golf.

What is the difference between other methods of playing golf and the method presented in this book? Why do I claim that golfing success results from playing God's way?

How my method evolved

Before I answer these questions, I must explain how my method of playing golf evolved.

As a member of the 501st Parachute Infantry attached to the 101st Airborne Division during World War II, I suffered a number of injuries in the invasion of

France. But these were minor compared to the severe injuries I sustained on September 17, 1944, the day our unit invaded the lowlands.

The invasion of Holland was in progress. As I prepared to jump from the plane, it lurched and I was thrown against the side of the door on the way out. Suddenly I found the parachute in front of my face and body. Frantically I attempted to thrust it away from me in order to secure its lifting force. In the same split second I was spun into the risers and suspension lines that secured my right arm and the reserve chute against my body. Looking down I could see the ground was approaching menacingly toward me.

Fear and anxiety gripped me. Frantic efforts to extricate myself failed. Death seemed certain and imminent. Two equipment bundles, each carrying three 81mm mortars, had been dropped from another plane. I was directly in their path toward the ground. One bundle came to rest on my shoulder; the other hung suspended below my feet. My fall to the ground was estimated to be 300 feet.

Fear gripped me

My platoon sergeant, Paul Wiltsie, later reported: "Bernardoni and I jumped from the same plane and on the same drop zone. After leaving the plane his parachute was collapsed by an equipment bundle. He was lucky enough to hang on and descend with only the equipment bundle chute sustaining him."

My parachute collapsed

Desmond Jones, a fellow paratrooper, recalled: "He hit the ground with this bundle landing on top of him . . . this bundle of approximately 500 pounds . . ."

The fact that I am alive today and playing golf proves the mercy of God. My thoughts turned toward Him. Suddenly I felt calm, confident. A peace which passed all understanding overruled all my fear. Somehow I knew that everything would turn out alright and simply relaxed my body.

Years later I related this experience to physicians at

the Mayo Clinic. They felt that the limp and relaxed condition saved my life. Had my body remained tense from fear, I would have been more severely injured or possibly killed.

Badly injured and pinned down by enemy forces, I remained on the front lines for 78 days. The ability to sustain pain for this length of time surely is a miracle from God. Paramedic Bill Grant taped me from the shoulders down to the sacrum and from side to side for greater support. Company commander Captain Jack Thornton and others did what they could to ease my excruciating pain and relieve me from front-line duty.

Relief forces finally came to our rescue, and I was taken to a hospital in Reims, France. Still encased in a body cast, I was flown to England where it was determined I had suffered a broken back. After being poured into another cast, I returned to the United States.

Eventually I was discharged, but after a few years, paralysis of the right leg developed. Examination revealed spinal damage from the fifth vertebra to the sacrum. A portion of the lumbro-sacro disc had become wedged in the spinal canal. An operation to alleviate this condition was performed. However, residual difficulty remains as well as other spinal ailments. Upon discharge from the Mayo Clinic I was told they had done everything possible for me. After a period of recuperation, marked by pain and determination, a semblance of normalcy began to return.

"Perhaps you ought to play the game of golf as a therapeutic measure," one physician suggested.

I accepted his advice. After much experimentation, I learned to hit the ball without pain. The therapeutic value has been invaluable. My enjoyment of golf developed to such a degree I decided to make the sport my career.

Manuel de la Torre, then assistant to his father, Angel de la Torre, professional at the Lake Shore Coun-

In pain for 78 days

Right leg paralyzed

Therapeutic value of golf

22

try Club in Glencoe, Illinois, helped me immensely. When Manuel left to become professional at the Milwaukee Country Club in Wisconsin, I became teaching assistant and later head professional at the Lake Shore Country Club.

Carefully I studied all the existing theories on positions, stance, swing, and follow through. I soon discovered that the information available in books, films and from professional golfers themselves did not take into account an individual's physical condition and limitations. Using principles I learned from Manuel and Angel, together with my own personal experience, I evolved a simple method which allowed my natural coordination to help as I struck the ball. Artificially induced methods failed horribly. When I experienced pain, I knew I had reverted to man's way—instead of playing golf God's way.

Playing with limitations

Though playing with spinal damage, I won the Illinois Senior Championship in 1974. This convinced me beyond a shadow of a doubt that playing the game with God-given coordination provided the key to success.

During recent years this method has proved itself. Regardless of physical handicaps, amateurs and professionals alike may enjoy the game of golf and do well at it. A man with one leg, another with one arm, and one who is blind, still another with a severely damaged shoulder as a result of a war injury—all find enjoyment at the game. Another with fingers missing from his hand, and one with severe arthritis and heart damage—these and many others amaze themselves and onlookers with their skill. If these can play a commendable game with physical limitations, nothing should hinder any reader from making the effort.

Even the blind play game

One of golf's all-time greats, Bobby Jones, once wrote *(Golf Is My Game;* Doubleday): "It seems obvious to me that writing about the golf swing has become too technical and complicated, and even the most earnest teaching professional presents the game to his pupil as a far more difficult thing than it really is. It is equally obvious that what the game needs most if it is to continue to grow in popularity is a simplification of teaching routines which will present a less formidable aspect to the beginner, and offer to the average player a rosier prospect of improvement."*

Divine wisdom aids technique Convinced that Jones spoke significantly on the subject, I seek to combine that simplicity of teaching technique with divine wisdom. Gracious testimonials affirm the success of this endeavor.

George Becker lost his right arm at the age of 8. Persevering against many odds and overcoming a host of handicaps, Becker today often leaves the 18th hole with a score of 77 to 83—a card most able-bodied,

----

*From *Golf Is My Game,* copyright ©1959, 1960 by Robert Tyre Jones, Jr. and reprinted by permission of Doubleday and Company, Inc.

George Becker

John McGough

two-armed, weekend golfers would be proud to show back at the office the following Monday.

John McGough has a congenital defect—no radius in his right arm. He has no thumb, yet plays golf well. In 1976 he lowered his score by ten strokes and now plays in the 80s. He has worked for the Wilson Sporting Goods Company for many years.

"I learned club control suited to my personal condition," McGough wrote me. "Although accuracy has always been my forte, your method has improved my distance considerably. It is a pleasure to watch the ball sail ten yards further than before I met you. Water hazards which were difficult to carry are a thing of the past. Thank you for making golf a pleasure."

One of the most remarkable golfers of all is Dave Meador. He is blind. When he steps up to the tee, he knows only by instinct where the ball is. He depends upon instinctive coordination to respond to his thought of sending the ball down the fairway, to the green, and into the cup. In 1974, Meador finished 8th in the National Tournament for the Blind with scores of 108, 110, and 115. He has scored many 18-hole rounds of 93 to 100.

He scores 93 without sight

What enables these golfers to overcome their physical handicaps and achieve respectable scores? It's simply a method which shows the player how to instinctively and automatically use the unique, individualized coordination which he possesses by nature. All mechanical theories are eliminated. It is not swinging the club as a professional or a friend swings it, but rather using the club as only *you* can use it. This I call "golf God's way." As you follow along, I think you'll agree it is the best way.

Understanding the Method

2

Many have sought help to overcome the strongest, most destructive force on or off the course—*fear*. When your mind is singular in its purpose, however, a calm confidence prevails. This confidence overcomes all fear of inability to perform physically, and overcomes external obstacles as well. The method I present is designed to help you overcome fear and develop confidence.

Use your computer-body

Simply, it begins with this basic fact: your mind is a computer. Your muscular system must automatically and instinctively respond without need of conscious control. All your needs, as a self-sustained organism, have been built into you by God. The problem comes when man tries to improve upon this God-given muscular system capable of flawless coordination.

Every golfer seeks the secret of maintaining a smooth swing for long accurate shots. Like most ardent golfers you probably have tried many theories to accomplish this. When one failed you went to another.

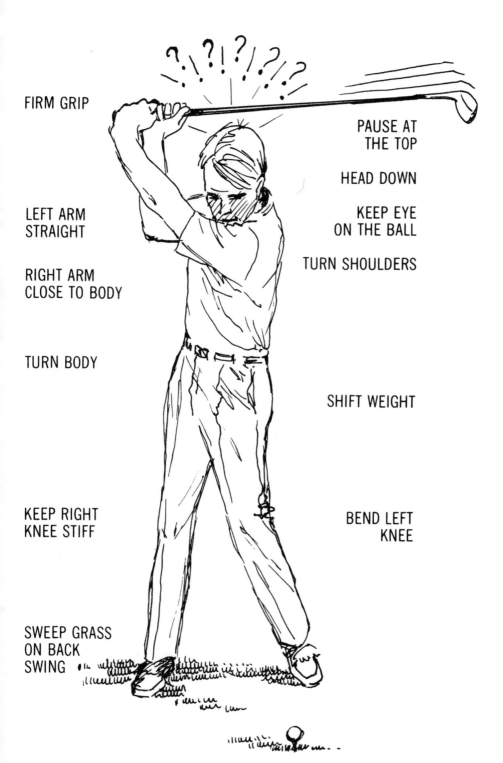

FIRM GRIP

PAUSE AT
THE TOP

HEAD DOWN

LEFT ARM
STRAIGHT

KEEP EYE
ON THE BALL

RIGHT ARM
CLOSE TO BODY

TURN SHOULDERS

TURN BODY

SHIFT WEIGHT

KEEP RIGHT
KNEE STIFF

BEND LEFT
KNEE

SWEEP GRASS
ON BACK
SWING

Many ask if there is a method one can learn which minimizes the number of controlling thoughts necessary to use any club effectively. My method has proved to be the answer many have been seeking.

Hundreds can be helped

Hundreds can be helped: those who have not been able to master keeping their head down and their eyes on the ball, left arm stiff, pivoting or shifting weight while at the same time making a proper shoulder turn, using legs and knees correctly, moving the left side out of the way while shifting weight, pulling down from the top with a stiff left arm, pressing the right arm into the side while keeping the wrists cocked in an effort to delay the hit, while at the same time keeping the chin behind the ball, keeping the back of the left hand towards the hole, hitting with the right hand while pushing the right side into the shot, having the right shoulder come under the chin, hitting against a firm left side, developing a full extension and turning fully into a high finish.

Are you confused? So am I. With that many details to keep in mind, no wonder most golfers need a simplified method for playing the game. Such a method is readily available for those who persevere.

The physical movements mentioned above are the result of the body coordinating to fit the purpose for the club in your hands. The purpose for the club, of course, is to hit the ball. Many times that purpose is hindered immediately upon arriving at the golf course. Upon stepping on the first tee, you conjure up mental blocks: an out-of-bounds shot, a lake, a stronger opponent.

Avoid mental blocks

Your desire to get off the first tee well, score decently and look good while doing so starts you checking your list of "dos and don'ts." You remember "point one" but forget "point two." In an effort to position your body correctly to produce a good swing, you paralyze the mechanism so it will not respond. Concentrating upon the mechanics diverts your attention from playing the course. This scattered attention often is the sole cause for badly hit shots. Your inability to pin-point the specific mechanical move causing your swing to fail develops tension. Inability to score well develops frustration, which leads to fear-paralyzing tension. Now the cycle is complete.

Let us assume you miss-hit the ball and it goes ten feet. What must you do next? Similarly, if you hit the ball well and it goes 300 yards, what do you do next? Some "experts" say, "Correct the error which caused the missed shot" and "duplicate the correct action." You cannot do either! You will find it difficult to pin-point your errors and you cannot consciously duplicate what you did right. However, you can hit the ball again. So if you miss the shot, simply hit it again. If you hit the ball 300 yards, hit it again. In both cases, the next step is the same: Hit the ball.

Secret: hit the ball

Set yourself free from the forces which hinder your good game. No matter how much you learn about the science of the golf swing, application of centrifugal force, mechanical movements and positions, pendulum action, or other details, your personal physical characteristics must be taken into consideration. Your muscular system, though complex, is automatic in its reaction and coordination. It is controlled by a superb computer—the mind—whose designer is God.

Muscular system computer-controlled

Thought of a desired action promptly stimulates a muscular response. For example, you decide to walk. The muscles of your legs and feet go into motion carrying the body along. You get out of bed, clothe yourself, have breakfast, get behind the wheel of your car and drive off. All of these activities demand reflex action from your muscular system. Did you issue direct muscular instruction for any of these activities? Have you any other habits in which you issue direct muscular instructions for performance and coordination? During these movements, did you control which muscle or group of muscles should exhibit greater strength over other muscles or which group should move before the other? Your vital life signs depend upon automatic response to thought. Why not golf?

You have watched an outfielder in baseball turn, run to a certain point, look over his shoulder and catch the ball. His muscular system automatically responded and coordinated for this purpose. He had no time to think what muscle should do what. He reacted to a thought stimulated by sight.

Muscular system responds to thought

As you jog along the road, you suddenly encounter an obstacle. Do you stop in the middle of your pace to consider how your leg muscles ought to be used, before jumping over, swerving around, or changing your pace to avoid the obstacle?

When a football player has his attention fixed upon the ball carrier, he will do his utmost to tackle him in spite of opposition efforts to block him. Instinctively he

wards off blockers, using his muscles to twist through an opening, drive towards the ball carrier and tackle him. All this happens automatically; instinctively.

Each individual has a unique way of performing. My own experience proved the point. I had learned and ardently practiced current golfing theories. But these movements could not be adjusted to my condition.

After many painful and frustrating hours of practice, I reverted to hitting balls as I once did while in a body cast and later in a back brace. Inability to bend my knees eliminated hip and leg movement. This caused me to focus my attention on the sole purpose of the club: to hit the ball. In spite of my physical handicap, I hit the ball well.

Focus on club's purpose

The more often I saw the ball fly straight to a target, the more I concentrated on using the head of the club correctly by moving my hands and arms. With no mechanical moves on my mind, I was able to focus upon the primary purpose—to strike the ball. Soon I noticed my hips and legs automatically followed this action. The arms pulled the shoulders which in turn caused the hips and legs to respond. The more I focused upon hitting the ball forward (left at the target), the more instinctive coordination moved my body the same direction. This eased the pain in my spine.

My purpose now is to present a simple explanation of the principles which stimulate instinctive coordination to produce consistently excellent shots. You need not be taught how to coordinate. You must be set free from erroneous and hindering thoughts which short-circuit the system. Your improvement will depend upon your acceptance of God-given laws. You must discipline yourself to trust the mechanism which performs everyday tasks, to perform equally well when called upon to use a golf club.

Accept God-given laws

I do not tell a blind man he missed the ball because he looked up. Nor do I tell a man with a permanently withered left arm to straighten it. It would not be wise either to tell a man with one leg to pivot or shift his weight.

The Word of God says you are what you think. "As a man thinketh in his heart, so is he." A thought held long enough will manifest itself physically. Science confirms this. The muscular system must respond to thought. It has no alternative.

Since the mind is always in the process of thinking, and the muscular system must respond to thought, reflect upon the ability of your muscles to accomplish that which you desire or visualize.

Review your thinking. Why do you have the club in your hands? What is your purpose on the golf course? Is it not to keep the ball in play, to get on to the green and into the cup in the least number of strokes? What role then, do you play in all this? You allow the body instinctively to coordinate with the action of the club. This is the correct sequence: the use of the club for a specific purpose first, controlled by your hands, the body moves instinctively.

What role do you play?

You accept without question the ability of your body to digest food and distribute nutrients; to respond automatically to messages from your eyes and ears; to correlate your vocal cords, mouth, lips and tongue to speak; your muscles to lift objects, twist and bend the body; to grow hair on your head, nails on your fingers and toes, and to pump blood throughout the body in fighting infections. All these responses, vital to life, are performed flawlessly. Why not in golf?

The Eyes

Many golfers tell me they have difficulty keeping their head down and eyes on the ball. You may have been told you missed the ball because you looked up. The truth of the matter is, you took your attention off

32

the purpose: striking the ball with the head of the club. Your eyes and head followed where you directed your attention. While talking with you, if I move to the left or right, you follow me with your eyes and head. If you take your attention, focus, purpose, or determination away from striking the ball with the club head and place it elsewhere, you will be accused of having "looked up." It isn't looking at the ball as such, or keeping your head down which you must develop, but a mental, singular, unswerving determination to strike the ball with the head of the club.

This attention, focus, purpose and determination will also direct your muscular system to use the club against the ball in synchronized timing.

Determination is the key

When driving an automobile, how many of us think about a hundred other matters rather than about the technique of driving? What stimulates proper physical response? Your eyes, of course. They relay to the brain the road and weather conditions, movement of traffic, automobile speed, traffic signals, children playing near the road, and countless other situations encountered while driving your car. These messages stimulate physical actions necessary for safe driving. Not once did you consciously issue instructions for muscular coordination. How can you place full confidence in this God-given computer to coordinate your body in handling two tons of fast-moving steel and not trust it to coordinate the use of a club head to strike a golf ball?

Your brain can receive positive or negative messages through your eyes. When a picture of a wide fairway, void of traps or trees, with no out-of-bounds or lake to cost a stroke, is received by the brain, a well-coordinated, synchronized action results. The ball is sent far down the middle of the fairway. A picture of a large green without problems brings the same results. You make a fine shot to the green and two easy putts.

What does your brain see?

After a few holes, however, your eyes telegraph a picture to your brain that an out-of-bounds to your left is threatening, that a heavy line of trees is on your right. The fairway is narrow with an easily-accessible trap. After four attempts, you find your way out of the trees. After a deep breath, you hit toward a well-trapped, elevated green. Several attempts in the trap finally bring you to the green only to face a fast, steeply undulating surface. After three putts, you find the cup. Do you recall the difficulty you had reaching the green of a par 3 hole on the first try because you saw water from tee to green?

How differently do you play holes? Consider how differently you played these holes. Was the difference mechanical? A loss of coordination? Evidence proves your muscular coordination was disturbed when the brain received negative messages from your eyes.

Proper messages from your eyes determine your muscular response. Remember how well you played after watching a well-known player practice or play? A pic-

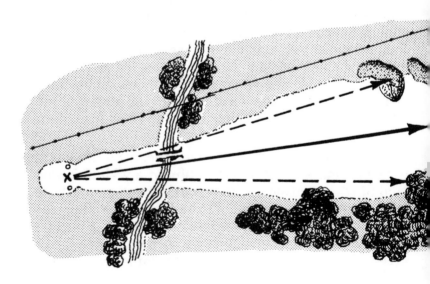

ture of the player's action was registered and you, temporarily, responded without fear. You did not have a hundred other thoughts, but a picture of his over-all motion. The body always responds to the club, not the club to mechanical moves.

Make certain your eyes send positive messages to your brain—about the fairway, the green, and any area in which a possible error can safely be made. See the green, not the trap or the lake. Allow your eyes to help in the club selection. They are the world's finest range-finders. Only when hampered through fear, anxiety, concern, or worry, will they be unable to send a correct message. Focus your eyes on the successful end results. Your eyes, also, will automatically telegraph the amount of impact necessary to send the ball a given distance. When your eyes see a short distance, you instinctively respond to hit the ball that distance. When your eyes see a greater distance, you instinctively respond to hit the ball that distance.

Where to focus your eyes

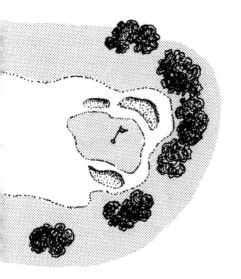

MAKE CERTAIN
YOUR EYES SEND
POSITIVE MESSAGES
TO YOUR BRAIN—
ABOUT THE FAIRWAY,
THE GREEN,
AND ANY AREA
IN WHICH A
POSSIBLE ERROR
CAN BE MADE.

35

The Ears

A baseball player disturbed by fans or opposing players is called "rabbit ears." Unless he guards against reacting to the sounds in the stands his ability will be affected. Olympic athletes have learned to exhibit total oblivion to disturbing sounds and influences, a discipline which is laboriously incorporated into their training.

Ignore sounds, influences

Golf should be no different. Often a touring professional is seen backing away from a shot or putt because of disturbing sounds. Such noises are evident in many sports. These sounds have hindered the coordination and synchronization of even the most successful athletes. Though sound may not send pictures to the brain to stimulate muscular response, it nevertheless can result in a calm attitude for a well-coordinated action or a stiff, jerky motion that leads to poor performance. Learn to close yourself in—to concentrate—when playing a golf shot. If this is difficult at first, practice holding your thought of a fine golfer and the business of playing golf for as long as you can.

Sound affects performance

Sounds from the wind can be a help or a hindrance to the golfer. Similarly, a voice you like or dislike can affect your play. Every sound causes a physical response. An airplane overhead, for example, will disturb many. What sounds can you relate to which have caused you difficulty? Become aware of this reality and guard yourself from their hindering force. You may lower your score by several shots in so doing.

Wind, airplane noises bother

Sounds often are noticeable under pressure or duress which may never disturb you under other conditions. You may be completely oblivious to sounds, whether playing alone or with friends, and play a good game in spite of a poor grip, address position, or whatever. Sound, along with negative impulses from your eyes, may magnify any mechanical error that weighs against a smooth, coordinated muscular response. You

36

should eliminate as many flaws—in your hand balance, address balance, and thought pattern—as possible.

Don't be eager to listen to an unqualified voice that guarantees you a quick solution to your slice or hook or tells you how to gain more power through gimmick movements. How many have you found who can coordinate alike, who are built alike? You cannot respond as another responds because you are not emotionally and physically the same.

No quick solution to your faults

Words which reach your ears are transmitted into thought which demands physical response. Learn which words stimulate a coordinated response from you. You will learn that words have a strong effect upon your overall reaction. Teaching is simply correct word usage—communication between the teacher and student. The teacher cannot teach you coordination. However, the teacher can provide you key words which trigger your coordination. Filter all sounds which enter your ears. Guard with all your might sounds and words which reach your brain. When you learn to refuse well-meaning advice or words which destroy your singular purpose to play golf or to simply hit the ball, you will be amazed how well you will score.

Words trigger coordination

The Fingers

When the hands holding the club are properly balanced, the fingers will sense the weight of the club head during motion and send their messages to the brain. The brain in turn signals the body for proper coordination and synchronization to the motion of the club. The only connection with the club is through your fingers, and their position on the club is of the utmost importance.

Correct hand balance and pressure stimulates correct muscular strength and response. We will elaborate on this in a later chapter. It must be understood that a tight grip causes tight muscles; sloppy grip, sloppy muscles. During a golf lesson one day I noticed that my student, a doctor, had a clutching, death grip on the club.

Right grip
key to success

"If you hold the scalpel in that manner, you'll never operate on me," I told him.

His response was immediate, "I hold the scalpel in this manner," indicating the pressure between his thumb and forefinger and the action performed with the scalpel. When the doctor applied similar pressure on the club he became sensitive to the weight and moved the club smoothly and efficiently for many fine shots.

You should use the same level of sensitivity to the weight of the club head as the surgeon does to his scalpel. As your eyes send messages to the brain, your fingers do likewise—messages as to the weight in motion and at which point of the motion the body should respond to assist the club in striking the ball.

A Unique Individual

As a total being, you are a uniquely computerized individual from birth. Your responses, coordination, and ability to grasp and apply thoughts presented to you—all are unique to you. Whether thought stimulation reaches you through vision or sound, your response to them is automatic.

No two individuals respond to given stimuli in the same manner. No two individuals are emotionally and physically alike. No two individuals possess similar strength or quickness of reflex. Regardless of these differences we all possess one thing in common—a *muscular system which automatically responds to mental stimuli to accomplish a desired purpose.*

You are not muscle alone. If mechanical excellence were the secret and muscle memory the key, all players

Mechanical skill
not enough

39

could ignore thought completely. The Palmers, Nicklauses, Millers and Players would play flawless, excellent golf under all circumstances and perhaps many would tie for first place in each tournament. When a thought, lack of confidence, or noise disturbs these fine players, however, muscle memory disappears.

If the action is mechanical, they ought to be able to push a button, turn off their thought, and play perfect golf. The opposite is true. Any mental disturbance or specific muscular thought foreign to their coordination results in a missed shot. A slight change in thought or disturbance will cause a drastic change in your physical response and result in a badly missed shot.

This method is based upon God's unchanging laws. When an impression reaches your brain and you totally accept it, your muscular system, and any other part of your body for that matter, will respond to that impression automatically.

Use club for singular purpose

Let me repeat: you should learn to use the club for a singular purpose—to hit the ball. Allow the way you are capable of coordinating to assist you in using the club for that purpose. Functions vital to your life, some of which you are not even aware and which you cannot see, continue daily. Fortunately, you have no control over these functions. They coordinate for health in every area of your body. The digestive process for different foods, for example, is remarkable. This process is easily hampered through emotion. The unfailing action of your heart; the balance of your glandular system; the infection fighting system—all are reflected in an outward picture of health. This condition of health results without any conscious control over the various processes.

Coordinated strength vital

Similarly, in your golf game the combined coordinated strength of your muscular system must be allowed to play its part in assisting the use of the club to strike the ball without conscious control. Trying too hard often stimulates effort which impedes natural movement. If you cannot even control the formation of mucus in your eyes or when and how they should blink, stop attempting to control individual muscular movements. Trust the natural coordination given you by God to accomplish your desired end result.

The Balanced Foundation

3

Balance is the key to everything we do in life. There is balance in rest and balance in motion. God has established certain fundamentals of balance which must be considered before you can understand the simple art of striking a golf ball with the club head. Your golf game depends upon proper understanding of balance.

Each individual must establish balance between the hands; a natural coordinating relationship between the hands and arms, their relationship to the body, and balance between the upper and lower portions of the body.

Right balance a "must"

As a result of this balance, you will be able to respond physically and coordinate with the club as it moves away from the ball, back against the ball, and into a finish. Instinctive coordination and synchronization of the entire body will result. Body manipulations or contortions will not be required to bring the club squarely against the ball.

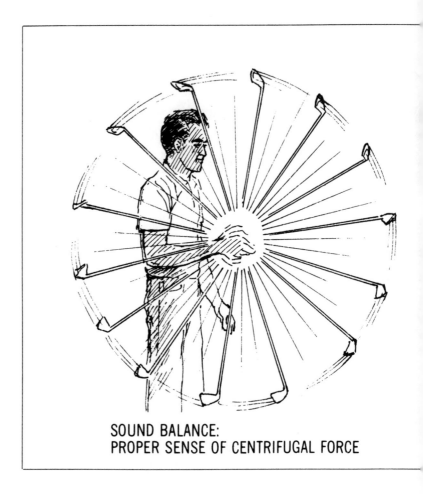

SOUND BALANCE:
PROPER SENSE OF CENTRIFUGAL FORCE

Every golfer likes to generate centrifugal force that sends the ball prodigious distances with accuracy. Proper balance permits your muscles to coordinate with the club head in developing this force. On the other hand, tension is present when you are not properly balanced in the address position.

When tension is wrong When you begin with tension you will increase this tension during the motion of the club, introducing a resistance against its force. You must eliminate the

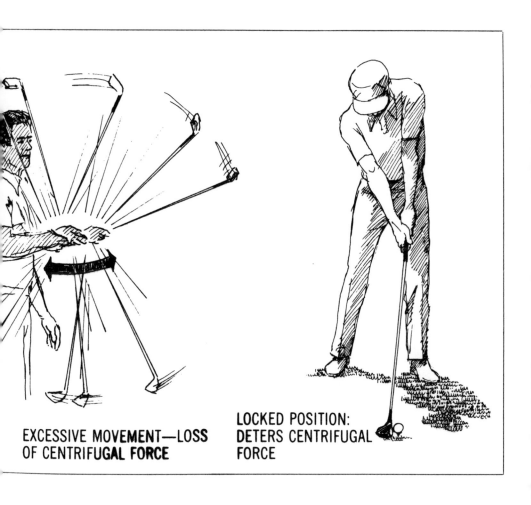

EXCESSIVE MOVEMENT—LOSS
OF CENTRIFUGAL FORCE

LOCKED POSITION:
DETERS CENTRIFUGAL
FORCE

slightest thought of brute force or stiffness which destroy coordination and increase muscular tension in the most critical area—impact.

Balance of the Hands

The hands are the connection between your club and your brain. When the fingers are properly placed on the club, they form a figurative electrical circuit to the brain. Your fingers, sensing the weight of the club in

Electrical circuit to brain

motion, telegraph messages of its whereabouts to the brain just as your eyes telegraph messages to the brain of road conditions while you drive your car. You will, in each case, experience instinctive and automatic responses to these messages.

Because of these automatic muscular responses to the weight of the club in motion through your fingers, many golf shots are saved in spite of your mind being hampered by *fear, doubt,* or *indecision,* any one of which is sufficient to paralyze response. Though you are not aware of these split-second changes which take place, your brain is capable of demanding physical response to these changes.

Fear, doubt, indecision bad

This does not mean you play by feeling—that is, conscious feeling. You actually play by instinctive thought only! There is a sensation of smoothness resulting from an unhindered physical response to thought. However, this is a result, not a consciously developed action. If you place your attention upon feeling, you cannot have your attention upon striking the ball with the club head or playing the course. Any feeling or sensation is recognized after the ball has been hit and is on its way. Though you may sense an error during some part of the action, the club is moved with such speed that at times you cannot adjust for it. Once the ball has been struck, it is too late to make corrections.

Adjust before striking ball

After futile attempts to pinpoint whether my ankles, legs, hips, feet, arms, elbows, wrists, shoulders, head or eyes were the cause of a missed shot, I decided to observe the position of the club in my fingers and the relationship of one hand to the other. When a proper relationship was established, I instinctively felt I could hit the ball without concern over my physical movements. This relationship stimulated a simple reflex action resulting in successful use of the club time after time.

How do you properly place the club in your fingers? Begin with the left hand. Allow the arm to hang at your side without tension, with the palm facing the thigh. Form a cradle with the tips of your fingers. Drop the handle of the club into your fingers closing them around the handle, placing the thumb and fleshy pad near the wrist joint on top of the handle. Make sure the club face is at right angles to the target—the line of flight—while resting on the ground. The thumb and forefinger must be opposite one another, forming an electrical circuit to the brain. The handle must rest deeply into the joints of the fingers, and all the fingers must remain on the club.

How to
place the club

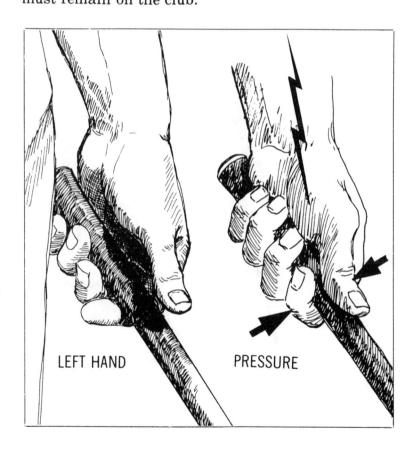

LEFT HAND   PRESSURE

Pressing the left hand against the thigh, you should simultaneously feel the thumb pad and the knuckles of the fingers. When one or the other is felt against the thigh, the left hand is not properly positioned on the club to fit the direction of the club face. All you need do

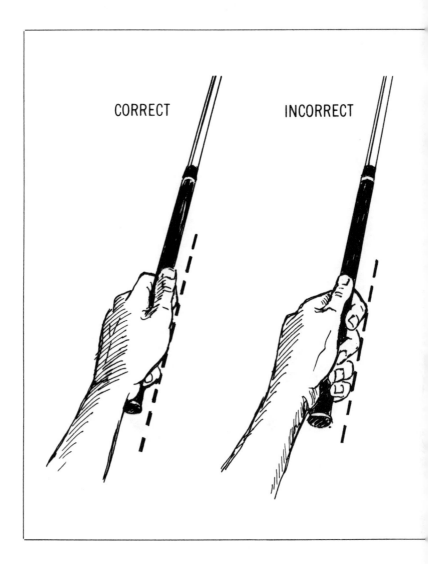

CORRECT   INCORRECT

is to have both thumb pad and fingers against the thigh and change the club face to the correct position. This alignment will allow the hands and club face to move in the same direction without adjustments or manipulations to place the club squarely against the ball.

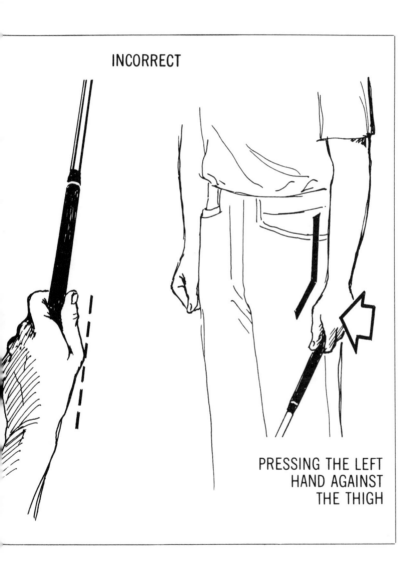

INCORRECT

PRESSING THE LEFT
HAND AGAINST
THE THIGH

You must also observe the relationship between the left arm and hand. As the arm hangs flexibly at your side, there is a straight line down the edge of the forearm to the base of the thumb joint. This forms an angle in the shape of an open *L* over the thumb forward. This is the natural coordinating relationship between the hand and arm which must never be altered when addressing the ball.

INCORRECT
RAISED WRIST

When placing the club behind the ball in this relationship, you will rest the heel of the club upon the ground and the toe will be raised slightly above the

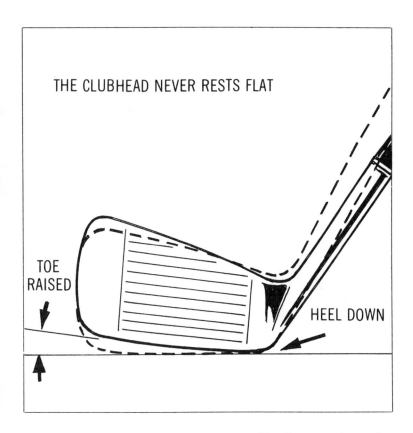

THE CLUBHEAD NEVER RESTS FLAT

TOE RAISED

HEEL DOWN

ground. The club never rests totally flat, on its sole, upon the ground. This relationship must be observed for all shots. Your hands will freely and accurately move the club in a continuous motion, squaring the face at impact without deliberate twisting and manipulating of the wrist joints.

Never—*never*—raise the wrist joint at the address to form a straight line from the shoulder, down the arm and hand to the club head. This has been the cause for many missed shots. When the wrist is raised in this manner you cannot begin club action properly. Body and hand manipulations result, and more often than not the hands must roll over the arm at impact. You will have difficulty squaring the face against the ball.

Watch that wrist joint

Now place the club deeply in the fingers of your right hand. This is accomplished by placing the groove made by the thumb pad and palm against the left thumb and folding the fingers around the shaft. Make sure the club rests in the cradle made by the first two knuckles of the forefinger while placing the thumb opposite the forefinger. This will place the thumb on the left center of the club. This relationship also forms a virtual elec-

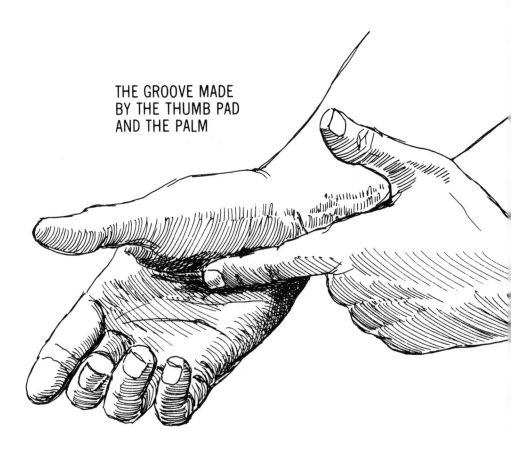

THE GROOVE MADE
BY THE THUMB PAD
AND THE PALM

trical circuit to the brain. These two fingers also send messages to the brain regarding the movement of the weight of the club head. This hand position will help retain left thumb position at the top as well as give you a strong feeling of power throughout the action. The hands are now properly balanced.

While the relationship of the thumb and forefinger of the left hand is up and down, the relationship of the

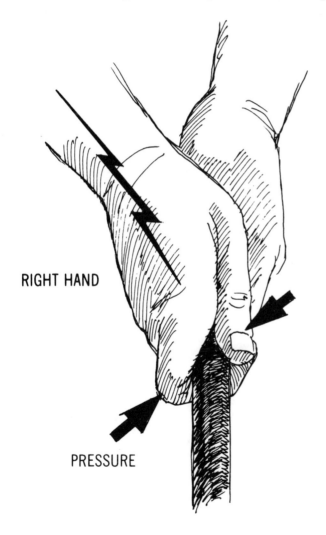

RIGHT HAND

PRESSURE

right thumb and forefinger is diagonally across the shaft. These fingers retain control over the club at all times, particularly at the top of the preparation for hitting the ball and at the point of impact. Since the right thumb and forefinger move the club against the ball, the handle must be against the side of the forefinger.

Finger control is important

Hands vary from individual to individual in size, strength and finger length, resulting in slight changes in finger placement upon the club. This deviation may cause the *V's* to point in a different line than you have been taught. Ignore the *V's* completely, allowing your natural balance to prevail.

Correct finger placement will make you acutely aware of the weight of the club. At first your fingers may feel weak in handling the weight. The more you handle the weight, however, the stronger your fingers

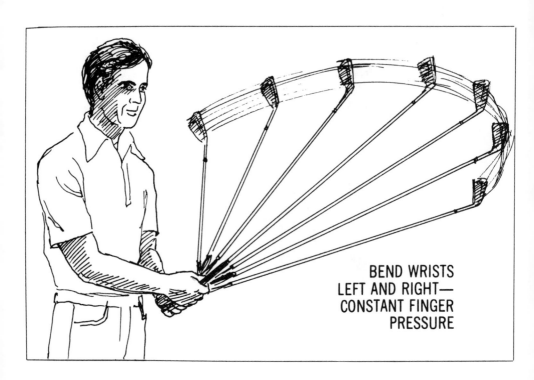

BEND WRISTS
LEFT AND RIGHT—
CONSTANT FINGER
PRESSURE

become and the easier it will be for you to control the club in action.

There are several ways to develop finger strength. Bend your arms at your side holding the weight above your hands waist high. Move the weight back and forth bending the hands at the wrist joints. Move the weight in a circular motion. Your fingers should never separate from the club while performing these exercises. Finger strength and flexibility of the wrist joints will develop, contributing to fluid club movement. The effect of these exercises will be felt in your fingers, wrists, and forearms. You can also strengthen your fingers by pressing or squeezing the tips of each finger against the thumb forcefully. This can be performed often. This strengthens the fingers in their grasp of the club.

Move weight in circular motion

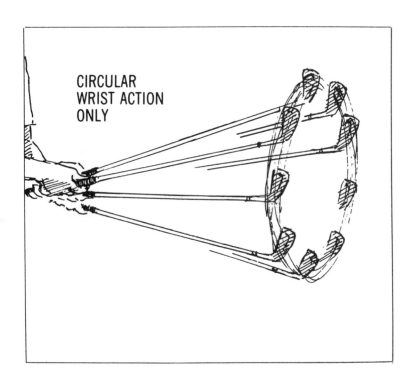

CIRCULAR
WRIST ACTION
ONLY

Which Grip is for You?

There are three grips involved in the game of golf: the overlapping, the full finger, and the interlocking.

The *overlapping* grip is achieved by placing the little finger of the right hand over or around the knuckle of the forefinger of the left hand. Those with short fingers will have difficulty placing the little finger around the knuckle and should instead allow the finger to rest upon the forefinger or use the full finger grip.

THE
OVERLAPPING
GRIP

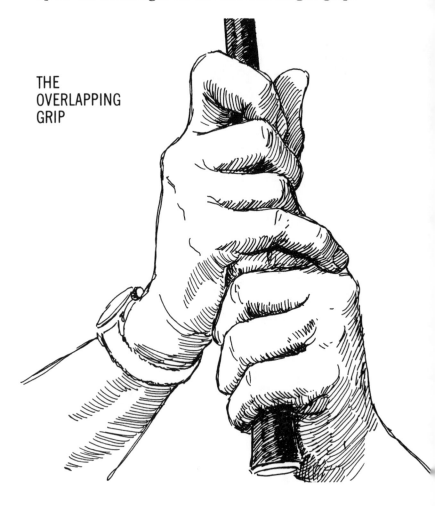

The *full finger* grip is used successfully by Art Wall, Jr., a topnotch touring professional. For this grip you simply place the little finger of the right hand on the club along with the other fingers of the right hand. This grip provides greater security and control for those with short fingers.

I recommend these two grips because they allow maximum flexibility of the wrist joints while retaining the pressure control points of the thumbs and

THE
FULL FINGER
GRIP

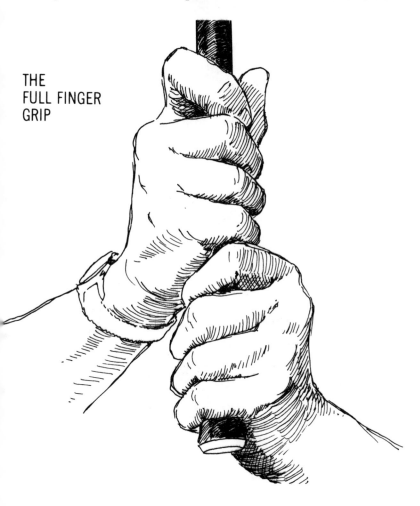

THE
INTERLOCKING
GRIP

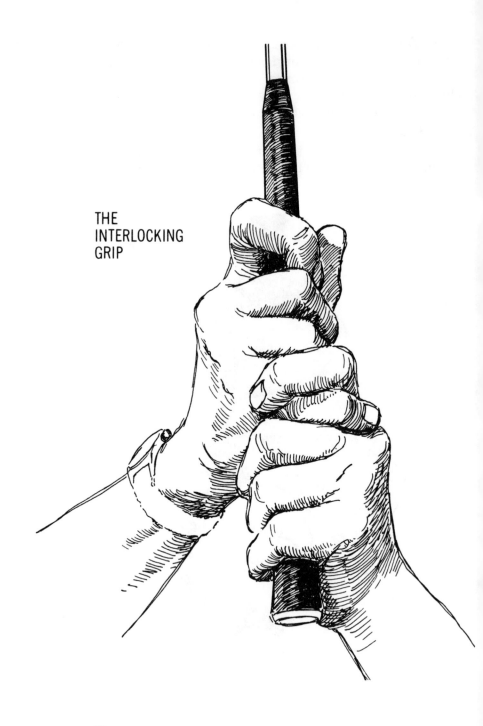

forefingers of each hand. These grips allow the hands to respond as one in controlling the club.

I do not recommend the interlocking grip because it hinders the relationship of the thumb and forefinger of the left hand. This grip demands that you squeeze the club with the last three fingers of the left hand, locking the wrists and stiffening the left arm. The right hand, in many cases, will be placed off balance to the left causing errors in handling the club.

Interlocking grip bad

You may already be using the overlapping or full finger grip. If so, check your grip against the hand positions mentioned in this chapter. If your grip is not the same, I would suggest you change your hand position for greater control and overall swing improvement.

Your grip change is worth suffering temporary frustration over missed shots for long lasting improvement and enjoyment of the game. Compare your grip with the correct grip. Is your right hand under or over the shaft? Is your left hand over or under the shaft? Does your body have to twist or contort itself at address in order to conform to your grip? If so, from this address position you will be hindered from coordinating with the movement of the club.

Is your grip correct?

The manner in which you hold the club affects the position your body will assume at address. When your hands are correctly placed on the club, your body balance will be correct over the ball. A change in your grip will result in an awkward feeling during the swing. This awkward feeling is not disturbing when the ball is not present. However, in an effort to hit the ball, you may revert to your old method of gripping the club. You must ignore these feelings until the new muscular response becomes familiar to you.

Don't revert to old method

When making a grip change, I suggest you wait until the end of the season, during winter months for those in northern areas of the country. The off season (if you have one) will give you sufficient time to adjust to these awkward physical sensations.

With the correct grip, take the club from behind the ball and place it hip high on the backward motion, away from the ball. The toe of the club should be pointing straight up. Return the club head to the front of

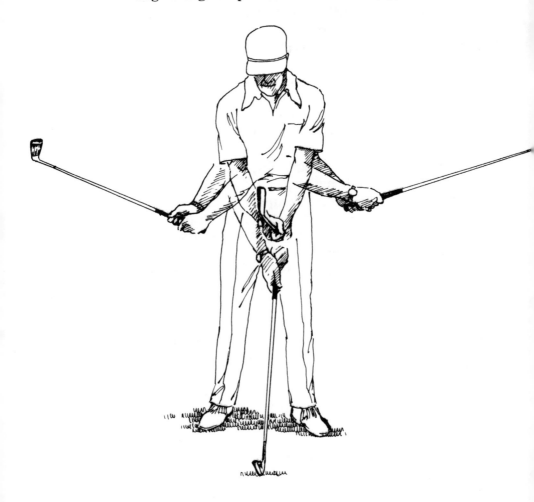

THIS PROCEDURE WILL ALWAYS PROVIDE A CHECK FOR CORRECT HAND BALANCE.

you, waist high, and place it once again upon the ground in front of you. If your grip is correct, the club face will be square to the line of flight when returned to its original position. You can perform the same movement in the opposite direction and the face of the club should once again be found square.

Place the club again hip high with your grip and check the club face. Is the toe straight up and down or twisted to one side or the other? Bring the club as it is in front of you waist high and then place it back on the ground. Is the face square to the line of flight? Is the face turned left (closed)? If so, you can see the possible result of your shot. Is the face turned to the right (open)? The ball may go right. This procedure will always provide a check for correct hand balance. Faulty hand position will demand manipulative moves from your body—instead of coordination from your body.

Place club hip high

Surgeon's Touch

How tightly should the club be held? How much strength is needed when the club is resting upon the ground? How much strength is needed to lift the club in preparation for striking the ball? In each case, very little. When the club develops centrifugal force, however, which pulls away from you and against the ball, you will automatically squeeze the club sufficiently to retain control. The fingers will never instinctively squeeze the club so tightly as to restrict or block against the club movement through the ball into the finish. Of course, you should not hold the club so loosely that the club handle moves in your fingers.

Centrifugal force developed

How much strength is needed to hold the weight of the club waist high? While holding the club waist high, have a friend try to pull the club away from you. What did you do? Automatically you tightened your fingers.

With the club in the same position, grip the club very tightly and have your friend attempt to move the club

The Balanced Foundation

to the right and then to the left. He will need to exert considerable strength to do so. A club held tightly cannot move freely through the ball, and you will have to muscle a dead club through the ball into the finish. Whenever the fingers squeeze the club this tightly the head of the club slows down. This tension not only locks the wrist joints and stiffens the left arm, but also will spread throughout the body. The controlling forefingers, thumbs and middle fingers of each hand will lose their sensitivity to the weight of the club.

When your grip is tight at address and remains tight to the top position, one of two things will occur: Your left arm and wrist will stiffen, preventing proper club positioning and rhythmic reversal of action, or you will loosen the fingers of the left hand, losing control over the club and creating countless errors in the downward movement towards the ball.

The finger pressure should be no greater than necessary to move the weight to the top position. This pressure will instinctively increase to the movement of the weight of the club when it settles into position, pressing the handle against the fingers. This is the natural—the correct response.

Mini Hit

The simplicity of taking the club head to hit the ball is best explained by illustration (see page 63). Place the club head waist high and have a friend hold his right palm against the face of the club. As in the previously mentioned movements, the weight of the club should be felt in your fingers. Move the club away from the palm with both hands bending at the wrist joints. Your arms move very little, if any, away from the sides of your body, keeping the fingers around the shaft at all times. Although both hands are united in their action, notice how the front fingers of the right hand play an important role in striking the club face against the palm with force and accuracy. These fingers exert the same

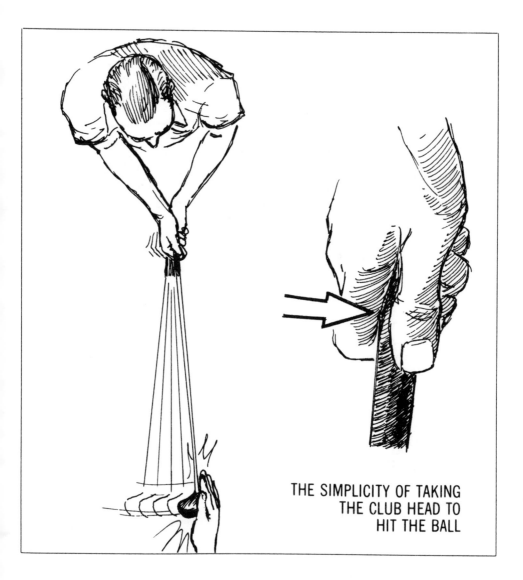

THE SIMPLICITY OF TAKING
THE CLUB HEAD TO
HIT THE BALL

control over the club face from behind the ball back against the ball. How simple can hitting the ball become? You just perform this motion on a larger scale.

While in the same waist high position, press the club face against the palm with continuous force. Notice once again how the forefinger and middle finger press the club against the palm. At impact it is these fingers which control the face for accuracy and power against the ball. Therefore, correct placement of the club in these fingers is of the utmost importance. Check the club position in your right hand.

Body Balance

You cannot hit hard unless your body is balanced. The foundation for this coordinated balance in motion is in the feet, legs, and hips. One way to destroy this balanced foundation is by placing the club upon the ground, bending from the knees first.

Never assume a sitting position deliberately. It places the spine in an awkward position, as those with spine or back difficulty soon learn. This knee position becomes easily exaggerated, causing the shoulder and entire body to turn more than necessary and resulting in an exaggerated horizontal plane of the club. The elevation you establish over the ball will be too low to allow the club, arms and hands to move freely. You will have to alter this position when attempting to hit the ball, thus increasing error. The body floats right and left, particularly from the hips and legs, eliminating proper turning coordination to the club. This position is fine for skiing, where a pumping action is required for balance, but not for golf. There is no terrain which demands up-and-down motion of your body as in skiing.

Sliding the hips right and left, as well as pivoting right and left, also destroys lower-body balance. While erect, slide your hips to the right, then left. Notice how the upper portion of your body dropped to the opposite side. Also, while erect, turn your hips right and left without turning your shoulders. Keep the chest facing forward. Notice that you can turn the hips without having to turn the shoulders. However, turn your shoulders right and left and you find it necessary also to turn the hips. This is the manner in which God created you. You

Feet, legs, hips bring balance

Avoid motion up-and-down

must adhere to His perfect order of physical movement, not some theoretical method. When you understand and accept this, you will be able to respond properly and will instinctively hit fine golf shots.

Using your feet, legs, and hips to initiate the movement will hinder coordination, centrifugal force, and timing essential for good shots. Initial movements

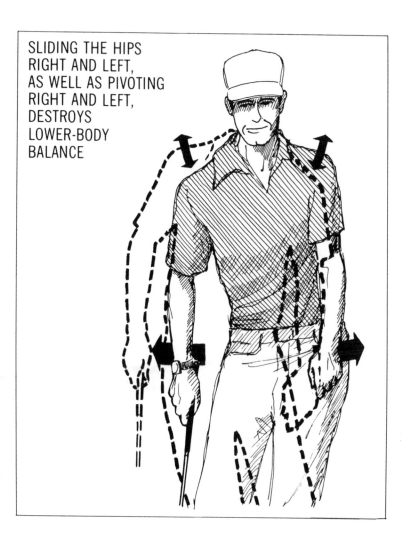

SLIDING THE HIPS RIGHT AND LEFT, AS WELL AS PIVOTING RIGHT AND LEFT, DESTROYS LOWER-BODY BALANCE

made by moving the knees right then left, bending one then the other deliberately and excessively, hinder balance in motion and destroy your foundation. Bending your left knee excessively causes the body to fall towards the ball and turn excessively right when performing the backward movement. Bending the right knee excessively when moving the club towards the ball causes the body possibly to fall to the right, fall

YOU CAN TURN THE HIPS
WITHOUT HAVING TO TURN
THE SHOULDERS (A).

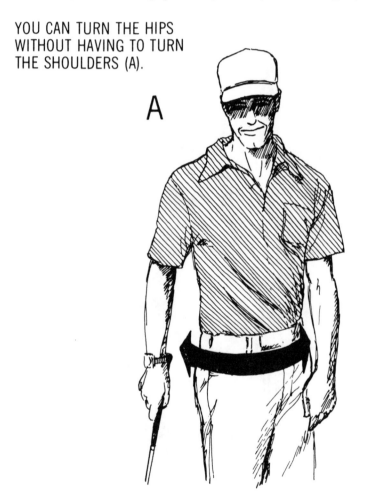

towards the ball, slide the body to the far left, or turn over the ball. You will also hit the ground many times when either knee is used excessively.

Turning of the hips deliberately, more than necessary, or shifting weight right and left will also destroy this balance. You cannot tell a man with one leg to pivot or shift his weight, yet this individual may hit the ball well.

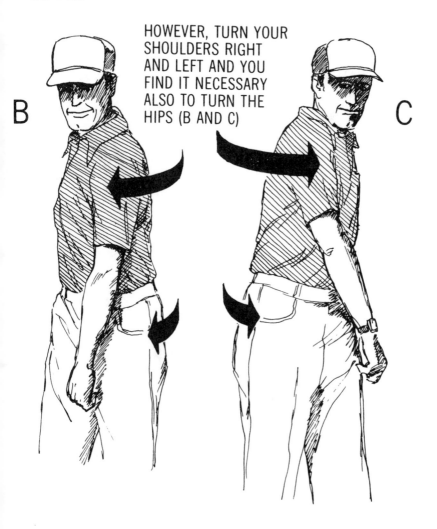

B

HOWEVER, TURN YOUR SHOULDERS RIGHT AND LEFT AND YOU FIND IT NECESSARY ALSO TO TURN THE HIPS (B AND C)

C

Correct Procedure for Balance

To see how it works, stand erect, arms loose at your sides and legs straight but not locked. Do not keep your knees deliberately locked or legs straight, but allow them to bend naturally. Bend from your waist as if to pick something off the ground or touch your toes. When your hands reach about the level of your knees or just below, there will be a natural desire to begin bending

THE NATURAL SEQUENCE
OF EVENTS

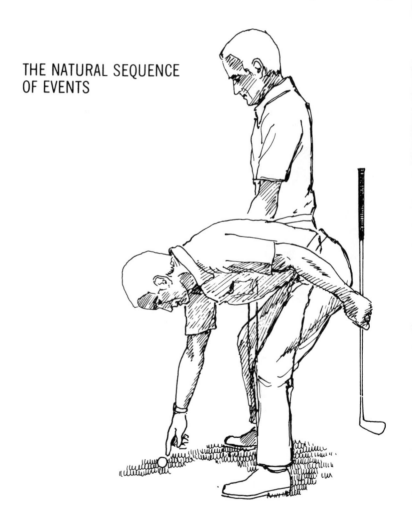

the knees. As you continue to bend over, you will continue to bend the knees until your hands reach the ground.

This is the proper sequence of events. Bending from the waist first demands that your knees bend to provide balance for the upper portion of the body, which has the greater weight. This is God's natural coordination in body balance.

Body balance
God's way

Do you wonder why you have missed so many drives? So many shots?

Since the above is the key to individual instinctive balance and coordination, how can you apply it to golf? Leaning your clubs against a wall will reveal a graduation in length from the driver down to your sand wedge and putter. Your woods have a slight graduation in length; however, they are the longest of your clubs. Numbers two, three and four are the longest of your irons. Many good players carry a one iron, which I do not recommend for the average player. Numbers five and six begin to divide between the long irons and the short irons, sometimes referred to as the accuracy irons.

The length of club chosen for the type of shot required to play will govern the amount of bending from the waist. When the club reaches the ground, you must stop bending from the waist. This establishes the correct relationship between the upper and lower portions of the body for perfect balance. This also provides the necessary clearance or elevation from the shoulders to the ground allowing the club, hands and arms to move freely back, down, and through the ball into the finish without changing your body level. To place the woods upon the ground requires little bending from your waist and knees. The longer irons demand slightly more bending from both. Your five, six, seven, on down to the sand wedge, will demand more bending from the waist requiring the knees also to bend propor-

Club length
affects bending

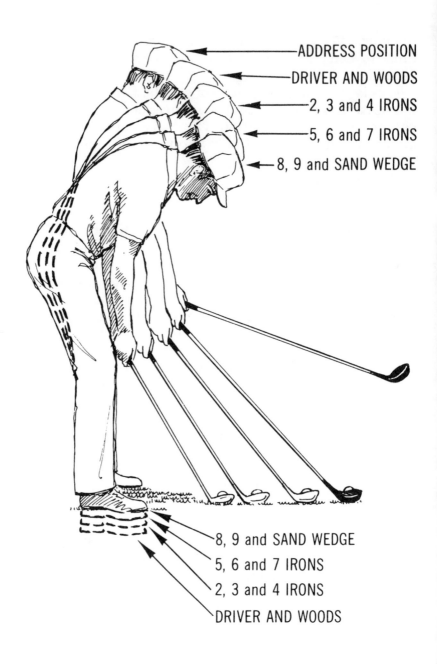

ADDRESS POSITION
DRIVER AND WOODS
2, 3 and 4 IRONS
5, 6 and 7 IRONS
8, 9 and SAND WEDGE

8, 9 and SAND WEDGE
5, 6 and 7 IRONS
2, 3 and 4 IRONS
DRIVER AND WOODS

tionately. The bending of the knees becomes progressively greater as you place the short irons upon the ground, balancing the weight of the upper portion of your body.

This foundation will balance the weight of the body in motion when coordinating with the head of the club to hit the ball. In other words, this balanced stance will eliminate manipulative moves from the body—no faulty shifting of the body, or unnecessary turning of the shoulders, and no lifting of the head.

Eliminate faulty moves

Resiliency Versus Tension

Never assume your address balanced position in a tense attitude. The same muscular elasticity present when standing casually must be exhibited upon placing the club upon the ground. From this position at rest, your muscular system must respond in this elastic, fluid attitude with the motion of the club. It is this muscular attitude which transmits strength and force to the crunching blow of the club head against the ball. It is this muscular attitude which stimulates coordination and timing at impact into the finish. It is this muscular attitude which stimulates the cat-like organization of the body at the top of the preparation of the club, and smooth reversal towards the ball. Stiffness, tension, rigidity, or anxiety at any point in your movement will cause problems of one kind or other.

Try muscular attitude

This elastic, resilient, muscular attitude is essential to use your club on the plane best suited for you. Your shoulders will be called upon to coordinate in this plane. The simplest way for you to understand the plane is to understand the angle your neck assumes when you bend your body from the waist. The club you select sets this position automatically. When you stand straight, your neck is vertical causing your shoulders to turn on a horizontal plane. As you progressively bend from the waist, the angle of the neck works towards

Coordinate your shoulders

The Balanced Foundation

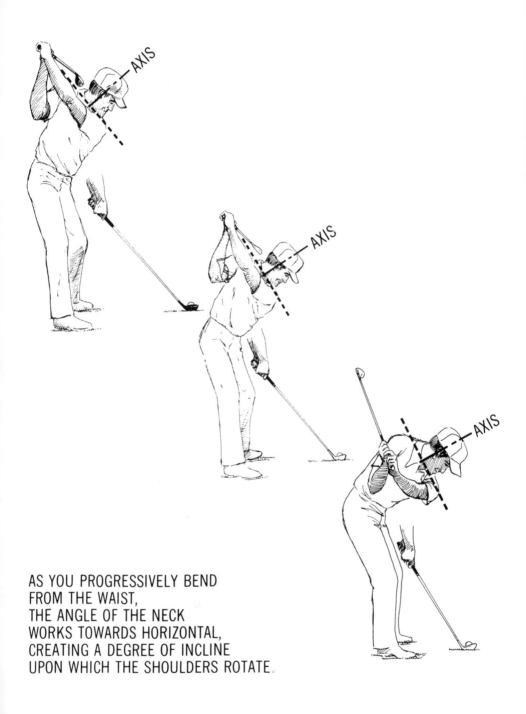

AS YOU PROGRESSIVELY BEND
FROM THE WAIST,
THE ANGLE OF THE NECK
WORKS TOWARDS HORIZONTAL,
CREATING A DEGREE OF INCLINE
UPON WHICH THE SHOULDERS ROTATE.

horizontal, creating a degree of incline upon which the shoulders rotate. Two extremes would be with your driver and your wedge or putter.

A forceful, speedy, anxious or tense move away from the ball will cause you to alter your position, your level over the ball. A stiff left arm may pull you to the right too much or push this center up at the top. Deliberately or accidentally moving the neck down, up, or from side to side, while moving away from the ball demands that you attempt to regain as closely as possible the original position over the ball in order to strike the ball accurately. Inability to return somewhere near this position results in a missed shot.

Move neck carefully

The center of action is the point between the collar bones at the base in front of the neck. When this center and neck angle are disturbed, the club and shoulders no longer have a center around which they can revolve.

Summing Up Body Balance

Your legs should remain ready to balance the weight of your body when your hands and arms bring the club to the point of impact. Your hands, arms, and club will demand coordination from the body whose weight will move during the action of the club. Your legs will bend at the knees and move towards the left automatically, responding to your intention to strike the ball to the target. Your legs should always be a balancing foundation for the upper portion of your body, coordinating to the use of the club. Your legs should never initiate the movement. Personal experience proved the point for me.

Legs will bend, move to left

Playing for therapy before and after the operation which fused my vertebrae, I studied and attempted all the modern theories in an effort to play good golf. The positions and calculated moves caused pain to shoot through my body. After months of pain, failure and frustration, I was ready to forget the game. Then I remembered hitting balls in a cast and later in a steel brace without pain. I began to hit balls without deliberate use of my feet, legs, knees, and hips. Not only did the pain subside, but the ball flew long and straight. I allowed the upper body to have all the freedom desired, moved only by my hands and arms. The upper body did not deliberately help the hands and arms, nor move excessively, but coordinated its movement to them. Deliberate and excessive body movement is extremely detrimental.

In a short time, the lower portion began moving to balance the motion of the upper portion. The stiff feeling began to disappear. My legs, hips and right side followed the hands and arms easily into the finish. I have taught this foundation of balance for more than 15 years and experienced astonishing success—both in my own game and in the games of hundreds of golfers, most remarkably with men and women who have a physical disability of one form or other. I am convinced this is God's way to better golf. It is available to anyone who is willing to exercise discipline and spend time in practice.

Balance: Arms, Feet, Ball Placement

4

The relationship of your arms and body is vital to proper balance and coordination during the action of the club. When you are standing, your arms hang flexibly at your side. You should have the same elastic attitude when you address the ball. This attitude must be maintained throughout the motion, allowing the pull of the club head at and through impact to straighten, not stiffen, the left arm. When your left arm passes the point of impact, it will bend to allow the club head to proceed into the finish.

On addressing the ball

The arms should never extend exaggeratedly outward from the shoulders when you are addressing the ball. A standard can be established by tucking the thumb of the right hand into the palm, spreading the remaining four fingers and placing them between your left hand and body. The error of standing too close is better than being too far from the ball. When you feel crowded, move away from the ball until comfortable.

Golf professionals often waggle the club head to sense the weight of the club in their fingers and thus to stimulate physical coordination to its movement. This preparatory movement prior to placing the club behind the ball allows your arms to remain elastic and ready to respond. This cannot be accomplished when the arms, particularly the left arm, are stiff.

Generating speed or force

The use of your arms in golf is far more important than you realize. The impression that speed or force cannot be generated without strong body or shoulder movement is not true. In order to use your arms to generate force against the ball, they must have a constant foundation upon which to work. When your hands and arms place the club in the preparatory position for striking the ball, they position the body for their support. When your arms have freedom to reverse toward the ball, they instinctively command the shoulders, hips, and legs to move into balanced position to assist the club head against the ball and into the finish. The large muscles of your body will help generate tremendous power. When your body is responsive to your arms, tremendous speed and force are generated at the bottom of your arc, sending the ball surprisingly long and true.

There are hindrances to developing this centrifugal force. Among them is hugging your rib box with the upper arms, by keeping your right arm against your side at address, on the way to the top, and pulling it against the side on the downward movement.

Don't hug your rib box

When addressing the ball with a stiff left arm, moving to the top position will increase its stiffness at impact, resisting the force of the club. This rigid, rod-like position of the arm causes other portions of your body to become tense, adding to the strain in hitting the ball. It will cause your body to slide to the left, dropping your shoulders to the right. If the body does not slide left, your legs may stiffen, keeping the body well behind the ball and causing you to pull down from the top, hitting the ground behind the ball.

Your hands cannot bend at the wrist joints and may roll over the arm at impact, closing the face of the club and possibly resulting in a shanked shot. You must try to avoid these hindrances to centrifugal force.

Try this experiment. Bend your left arm until the forearm is waist high and horizontal to the ground. Make a fist. Have your friend hold his right palm under the fist. Bend the arm upwards and strike a descending blow against the palm, exerting effort at the point of impact. Notice the force and power available to you.

Avoid hindrances

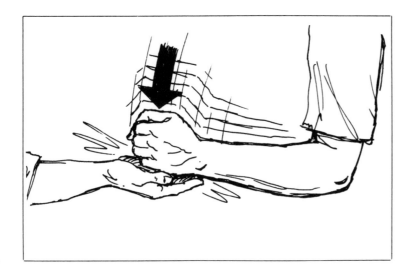

Try another experiment. Make your left arm very stiff, holding your fist in front of you waist high. Keeping the elbow locked, strike your fist against the palm in a downward blow. The lack of power is unmistakable. Strain can be felt in other portions of your body as muscles attempt to assist the arm to generate force. Attempting to use your club with a stiff left arm will produce the same results. You cannot move the club head faster than you can move your entire arm. Both of these experiments can be performed while holding your arm even with your left side.

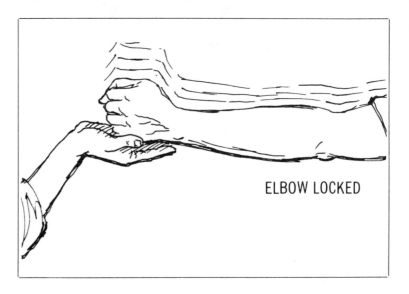

ELBOW LOCKED

Watch top touring professionals closely. You will notice a flexible left arm at the top of the preparation for striking the ball as well as at impact. In many cases a stiff left arm actually causes faulty body positioning and contortions.

The right arm should be in front of your body at address. Follow the club away from the ball freely and separate from the body when the club reaches the top. In its return toward the ball, the right arm glides in front of and close to your body, allowing the hands to **Keep right arm close to body** create a lightning attack of the club against the ball. All shots should be played this way. When both arms are in this flexible attitude, maximum speed—which is unhindered centrifugal force—can be repeated. There will be no hindrance to the club moving through the ball to the finish.

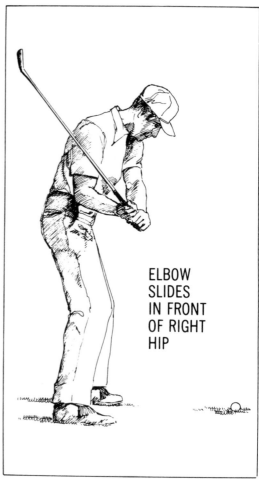

ELBOW
SLIDES
IN FRONT
OF RIGHT
HIP

For simple proof, place your feet together and restrict the use of your knees and hips. From this position, with your arms flexible, calmly move the club away from the ball, taking a long count to return to the bottom of your arc and striking the ball with force. Notice how the entire mechanism generates impact at this point sending the ball farther than you expected. When your arms are allowed free movement from the shoulder joints, you will remain balanced at all times. Practice until you can easily hit the ball well and long. To time the use of the club where the ball rests demands mental discipline rather than mechanical excellence.

You will lose your balance if you attempt to generate speed on the way down, manipulate your body for power, shift or pivot your weight away from the ball or toward the ball. You will discover that free hand and arm movement can result in hitting the ball at the point where the ball rests, at the bottom of your arc, with tremendous force and without body work.

One leg
no handicap

An individual with one leg can hit the ball a good distance without benefit of a straight left arm, body power, or weight shift. He proves that when a club head is handled in a flexibly coordinated motion, it is possible to hit the ball with lightning action and not lose balance.

Most professionals go through these movements so automatically and remain so well-balanced they appear to hardly hit the ball. They are not hitting the ball easily or sloppily. When every muscle is coordinated to the motion of the hands and arms they can hit hard without losing balance. Any portion of the body that resists this coordination—such as hitting against a strong left side, straight and tense left arm, big shoulder turn, or keeping the head down—will result in disaster.

Placement of the Feet

Good balance demands good footing. How far apart you should place your feet will depend upon your physical stature. You must experiment to find which stance is best suited to you. The width should easily accommodate the movement of your body weight. A narrow stance is more desirable than a wide stance. Too wide a stance will cause your body to sway from side to side and destroy coordination at impact. As a general

A NARROW STANCE IS MORE DESIRABLE THAN
A WIDE STANCE.

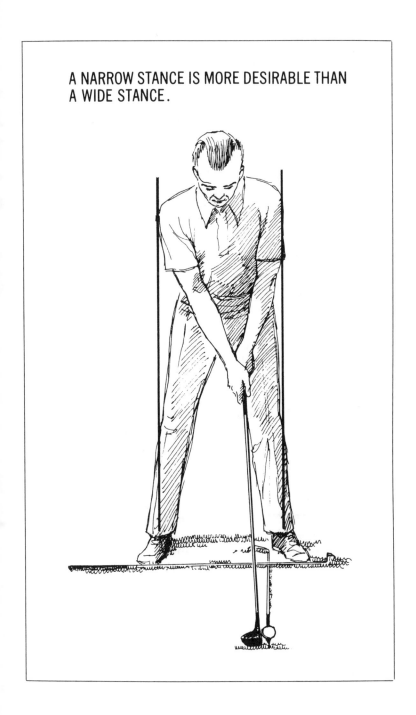

rule, place the heels the width of your shoulders.

You will time your shots much better if the heels are not lifted high off the ground during the motion of the club. When you lift the left heel, the return motion may cause you to fall left or back, twist the body too much, or move into an off-balance position.

Lifting the right heel off the ground as you near impact may cause a missed shot. This lift can push the body up, collapse the right side if the knee bends simultaneously, or turn the right side too much, rolling the right shoulder over the ball and forcing the club out and around the ball. Foot movement and heel lifting (which normally are very slight) must be an automatic reaction to body weight in motion, not a deliberate movement. Stop all toe dancing. Do not place your weight on the inside, outside, toes or heels of your feet.

Avoid lifting right heel

You should feel the weight of your body entirely on both feet. Otherwise you cannot begin your action on balance and will find it difficult to retain continuity of motion. In order for the body to move into position to assist and balance toward the force of the club head, it must have a sound foundation upon which to work.

The proper placement of your feet serves two purposes: to support the weight of your body in motion and to allow coordination through the ball into the finish without hindrance. Correct positioning of your feet can be achieved in this manner. Draw a line on the ground to the target. Stand at a distance from this line—whatever is demanded by the club you use. Draw another line parallel to the intended line of flight. Place your feet so the toes touch the line. Both toes should point directly at the line. Turn your right toe slightly to the right while turning your left toe much more toward the target.

Position feet correctly

Some feel they turn the toe about a quarter of a turn left. When the right foot is turned slightly right, it keeps the body from making too much turn to the right. Turn-

82

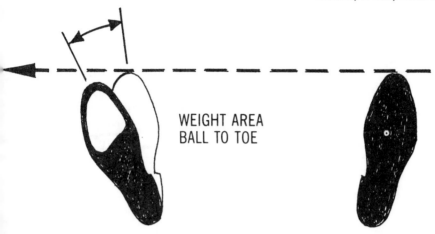

WEIGHT AREA
BALL TO TOE

ing your left foot provides a foundation from the ball of your feet to your toes, to accept the weight of your body coordinating with the club head through impact into the finish. This is the natural way to balance. The importance of a correct foundation cannot be overemphasized.

To understand and feel the difference in body coordination as a result of pointing your toes, particularly your left toe, place your feet against the line as before. When your left toe is pointing toward the line, the only

WEIGHT ON
OUTSIDE EDGE
OF FOOT

portion of the foot which can accept the weight of your body in motion towards the left is the outside edge of the foot. Inability to accept and balance your weight in motion causes your left leg to stiffen and your left side to resist as your body turns through the ball.

Your hips may lock into a position when sliding left, tilting upwards, causing your shoulders to fall to the right, or turn over the ball. Inability to coordinate through the ball will cause you to stop the club half way between the ball to the finish. You will have to manipulate your body to complete an otherwise easy motion.

Ball Placement

Correct placement of the ball in your stance, obviously, is important in hitting the ball to the target. Correct placement should also make it easy for you to **Place ball** see the line of flight. Place the ball in line with the left **correctly** heel. You can see the back of the ball and by turning your head can easily see the intended landing area.

When the ball is placed in line with the left heel, the club will arc directly toward the ball from the top, move toward the direction of your target, and continue easily into the finish. *This ball position should be used for every club—from the driver down to the wedges.* Is your short game erratic? Check the position of the ball.

Everything discussed thus far is for the purpose of balancing you for striking the ball. Arm relationship, hand balance or placement of your feet should not be considered as separate units. They are a single unit of balance for the purpose of efficient coordination to play a fine game of golf.

When you place the ball in the center, or back of center, in your stance your eyes cannot see the back of the ball and will direct the club either toward the ground behind the ball or to the top of the ball. The club from the top proceeds toward the ground in an effort to strike the bottom of the ball. When a strong downward force is applied toward the ground, you might stiffen your legs, force the body to the right of the ball, and

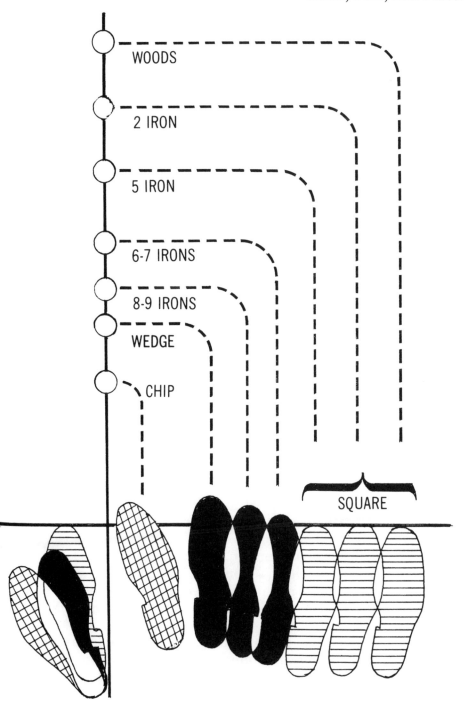

WOODS

2 IRON

5 IRON

6-7 IRONS

8-9 IRONS

WEDGE

CHIP

SQUARE

manipulate your body to bring the head of the club against the ball. If your body moves left, as it should, you will top the ball. How can you get the club against the back of the ball when it is moving toward the ground? Never place the ball at center or toward the right foot for any shot.

The more you remain on both feet at the time of impact, the better you will hit the ball and the farther it will go. The more you feel body weight on both feet—not on the right and then left—the more the large muscles of your body can move with coordinated strength to assist the club head against the ball. During the course of hitting the ball, your hips will move normally left while the head remains in a centralized position. Though the weight is moving left, the right heel does not lift until after impact and moving into the finish. When your weight is on both feet, the shoulders are able to circle around your neck—the hub—moving the hips left and causing the legs to move over to balance this motion. This keeps your head over the ball for a longer period of time. As long as you remain balanced from the hips down, you will always be balanced in motion.

A circular action demands balance. You cannot have balance in your swing when your feet move excessively. A balanced foundation is the key for good golf.

A Helpful Exercise

Here is an exercise that will help you develop overall correct muscular coordination. It can be performed only when you remain solidly upon your feet. As you become proficient, you will notice that the feet are moved as a result of the way you move your body instead of moving your legs and feet to stimulate body motion.

Take a club in your hand, preferably a three wood or long iron, and assume the address position. Without straightening up to an erect position, hold the shaft of

Feel body weight on both feet

Moving body affects the feet

DURING THE COURSE
OF HITTING THE BALL
YOUR HIPS WILL MOVE
NORMALLY LEFT
WHILE THE HEAD
REMAINS IN A
CENTRALIZED POSITION

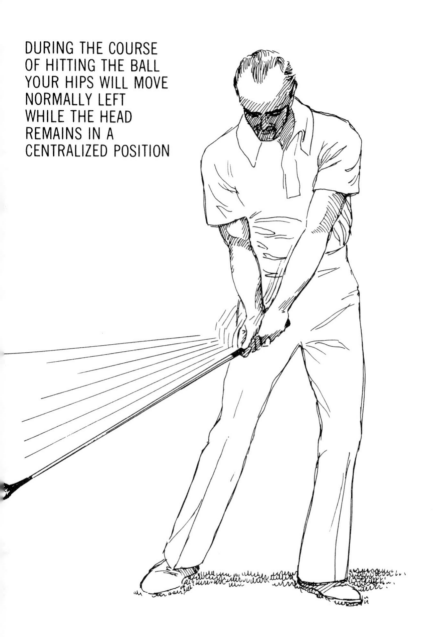

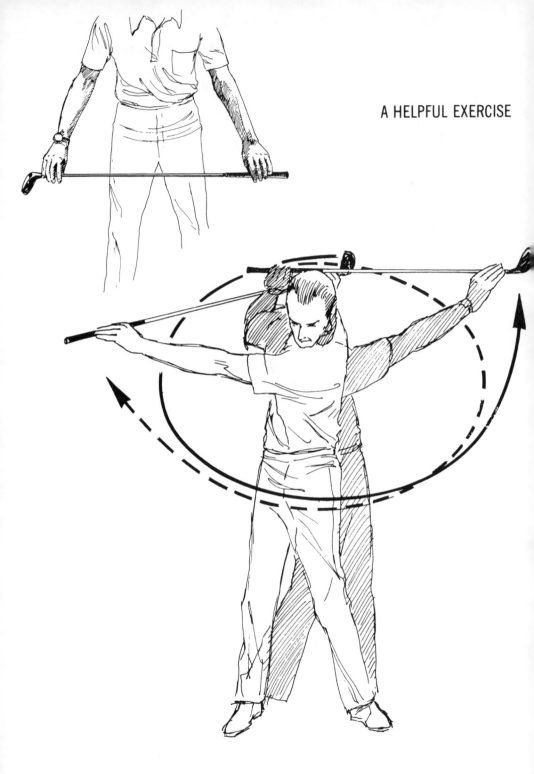

the club in the tips of your fingers, about 30 inches apart. Take the club and place your right hand and arm over your right shoulder. The upper arm is horizontal to the ground while the forearm and wrist are bent backwards toward the shoulder. The left hand and arm stretch to the right, *shoulder high but do not stiffen. Never stiffen the arm which stretches.*

Reverse this procedure to the left. The left upper arm is horizontal to the ground while the hand and forearm bend backward toward the left shoulder. The right hand and arm now stretch to the left shoulder high *without stiffening.*

Your eyes choose a spot upon which to focus. The head turns, but your eyes remain on that spot. The body must not raise up from the original position. Allow the feet and legs to move as they are called upon. Move the club from side to side smoothly and calmly. *Never practice this exercise with tension, speed, or body thrusts.* The arm which stretches moves to a horizontal or shoulder level only. This stretches all of the muscles necessary for overall coordination. This is a good exercise for the waistline as well.

Notice how well you balance your body weight in motion with the use of the club. This is synchronization. This will strengthen the muscles necessary for golf. Notice how your feet move as a result of your body weight in motion. At first you may have some difficulty, but keep at it and soon it will become second nature.

Bend wrist
backwards

No tension, speed,
body thrusts

Natural Preparation for Hitting the Ball

5

Have you seen a cougar, tiger, leopard, lion, or other cats as they prepare to leap upon their prey? Did you marvel at their smooth, synchronized, well-coordinated muscular action? Would you like this same smooth, flexible movement of muscles for long accurate golf shots?

There are strong and weak, large and small cats. However, they all instinctively respond to stimuli—a purpose—without conscious muscular control. You should also. They use individual coordination and strength. You should also.

Respond to stimuli

Successful athletes respond to stimuli as instinctively as these cats. There are strong and weak, big and small athletes. Regardless of size or strength, all athletes have a purpose for action before assuming the ready, or beginning position.

A baseball player looks at a coach for signals before assuming his position at the plate. His position will be for the purpose of bunting, hitting behind the runner, hitting to right or left field, or attempting to hit the ball for the fence. All these athletes carefully prepare themselves to perform to a purpose. To successfully accomplish their purpose, athletes in these and all other sports assume an aggressive attitude. This includes golf.

Your purpose in golf is to strike the ball with the head of the club and get the ball on the green and in the cup in the least number of strokes. This purpose should always be uppermost in your mind when addressing the ball, regardless of the club used.

Strike ball with club head

The purpose of this chapter is to teach you how to position yourself in this cat-like, ready-to-attack position to strike the ball.

Before assuming your balanced address position, consider which area of the fairway affords the greatest margin of error and the best position from which to hit to the green. For your second shot, determine the best entrance onto the green, what portion of the green you should hit the ball to and which club is best for the shot.

Unless these questions are definitely answered prior to addressing the ball, you may be inclined to use manipulative moves to compensate for fear or indecision. The error you feared will result, not from inability to coordinate or control your club, but from confusion. These factors have a subconscious effect upon your body position or balance over the ball. Begin your round properly. Calmly decide how you can best attack the course, choose the club for each shot and calmly prepare to hit the ball accordingly.

Confusion causes error

Many misinterpret this purpose and aggressive attitude. Through acrobatics, manipulations, contortions, or pretzel twisting moves of the body, they mechanically prepare themselves to hit the ball.

Subconscious reaction to your purpose directs body members to place the club head behind the ball, without fake motions. A flexible, ready position will result. Your body will face the ball squarely. It is your natural ability to respond which enables you to make a good shot—one that will be the first of several to achieve the ultimate objective of putting the ball in the hole with the fewest number of strokes.

How to Prepare the Club to Hit through the Ball

A baseball player places the bat back to his side without a stiff left arm, shoulder turn or pivot, long extension, etc. He prepares his bat to use against a pitched ball. Turning away from the pitch would take his attention and sight off the ball, destroying his ability to adjust to the level of the pitch. Prior to assuming his position at the plate, he checks with a coach for signals as to his purpose at the plate.

How do you achieve the balanced position illustrated in the picture on page 90? The body firmly balanced over the ball, hands correctly positioning the club at the top preparatory to hitting the ball, left arm reaching back, slightly bent (not stiff) left knee properly bent—without thinking about the mechanics?

First of all, remember to place the club on the ground, retaining the relationship of your left hand and arm. This is vital, otherwise your hands cannot begin the motion correctly. The toe of the club is slightly raised off the ground. Having positioned yourself over the ball ready to respond to the purpose (to hit the ball), your thoughts will be of the utmost importance. Think calm; think natural response; think relaxation.

At this point you must also understand the freedom of motion the arms have at the shoulder joints. While standing erect, swivel your left arm in a circle. Was your body required to assist this movement? Your body provided a foundation for the motion of the shoulder joint. The shoulder did not move the arm. To stimulate this action, you used a simple thought—*circle the arm.*

Natural Preparation

No direct, individual, muscular instruction was issued. This understanding will be of the utmost importance when positioning the club at the top—the preparation for striking the ball.

Assuming you have positioned yourself over the ball properly, as described in the chapter on body balance, you are ready to learn how to "place" the club in the preparation position for striking the ball. *Your hands calmly take the club from behind the ball and place it in the preparation position shoulder high to strike the ball.* This calm attitude eliminates any quick movements, stiffness or anxiety, allowing you to retain an aggressive attitude toward the ball and target. This calm attitude helps produce a well-balanced preparatory position with your body weight on both feet ready to assist the club against the ball.

Calm attitude essential

When addressing the ball, your arms should hang flexibly from your shoulders. Stiffness or tension should be avoided at all costs. The hands should place the club shoulder high. Never place the hands above shoulder level. Both arms follow the hands, using the shoulders as hinges.

How does your body properly position itself? As your hands approach shoulder level, they pull the left arm which positions your left shoulder in front of your chin, twisting the hips right, straightening your right leg and automatically bending your left knee. Normally the shoulder stops in front of you. When this sequence of movement is followed, no excessive muscular response will be experienced. Your left arm will not be stiff, your shoulders will not turn more than necessary, your left knee will not bend excessively causing you to collapse your left side, nor cause undue manipulation toward the ball. Your body was not needed to assist your hands and arms to prepare the club for hitting. Your hands and arms move independently from the ball to the top signaling the body when to coordinate to

No extensive muscle response

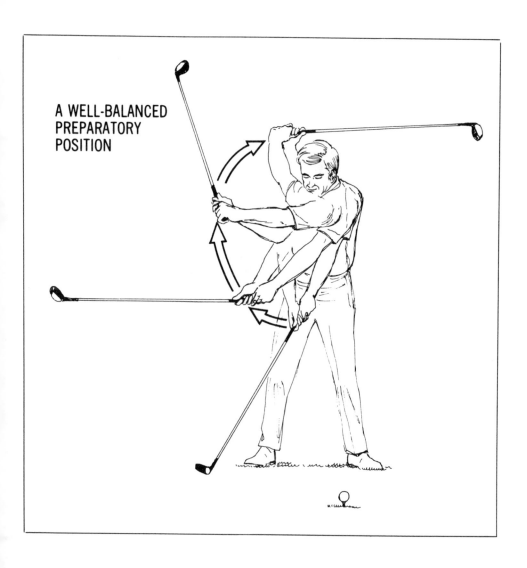

A WELL-BALANCED
PREPARATORY
POSITION

their motion. Your body has properly positioned itself.

Never place the club in the preparatory position by dragging the club away from the ball, with strong muscular movement, stiff arms (the erroneous thought that the faster you move the club up, the more speed you have in your stroke), arm or shoulder push, etc.

To swing naturally your weight must be equally on both feet. Why lose balance pivoting and shifting your weight? Why practice deliberate turning of your shoulders and hips? It is impossible not to turn your shoulders when placing the club to the top. It is equally impossible not to turn the shoulders, hips or legs when the club strikes the ball, with centrifugal force pulling you to the finish.

On turning shoulders, hips

When the arms climb too high, they separate too much from the body and will have a difficult time catching up to the body on the way down. Lifting too high can be caused by a stiff left arm, forcing your head up as it lifts the left shoulder, bending the body toward the left, or locking against your chest because you are attempting to remain in position with your head.

A golfer who is well-muscled around the chest, shoulders and back should never place the club very high. Excessive movement of the club will cause this individual to lose coordination. Instead he should place the club between the waist and shoulders. From this position the hands, arms, club, and body are ready to respond in a unified effort through the ball into a higher finish.

Do not turn your body too far right, possibly into an off-balance position. If you have not been able to finish full and straight, check your turn away from the ball. *You need more wrist work than body and arms.* The force you have available to you in this action will amaze you. You should practice making a short motion away from the ball and a large motion to the finish.

Body turn affects balance

Do not lower your left shoulder when placing the club in the preparation position. Proper elevation has been established when you place the club on the ground. Therefore, the hands will bring the left arm up to your chin as they move the club away from the ball. Many errors are made by attempting to get the left shoulder

96

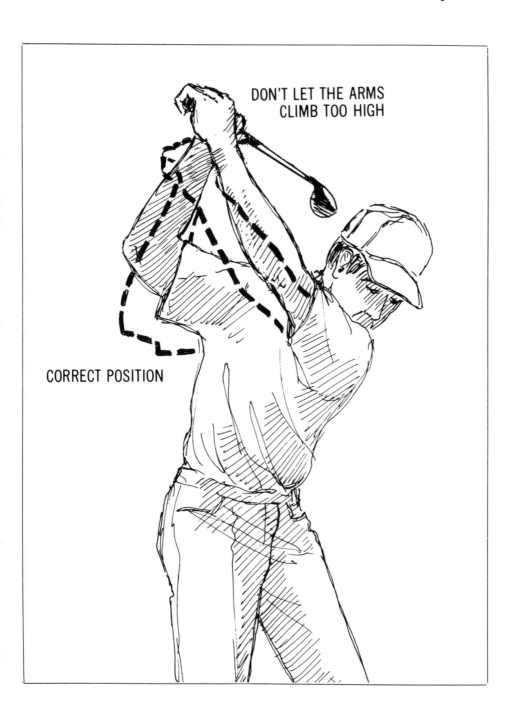

DON'T LET THE ARMS
CLIMB TOO HIGH

CORRECT POSITION

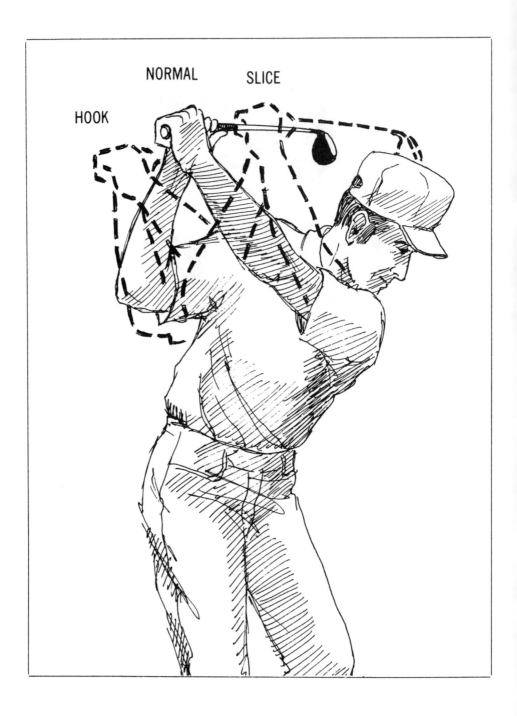

HOOK NORMAL SLICE

under the chin. This bends the left knee unnecessarily, collapses the left side and causes you to fall right and over the ball, demanding similar movements toward the ball.

Calmly placing the club in the preparatory position as described will teach you the best position for hitting the ball squarely. Don't place the club higher than your right shoulder. This will vary according to physical build and dexterity. If the ball is fading, place your hands more to the back of you. If hooking, place your hands more to the front of you. You can hit the ball from any position. As you can see, physical limitations are no barrier to hitting the ball.

Anyone can use this manner of hitting the ball, regardless of physical build or one's ability to coordinate. Your desire to hit, bang, or strike the ball will not be hindered. Remember, golf is as aggressive as any other sport. A bat is used in baseball, a racket in tennis. In golf, one uses the head of the club aggressively. Therefore, a calm attitude in placing the club into the preparation position for striking the ball is imperative in order to reserve all force against the ball. Practice the balanced position for striking the ball until you can place the club from address position without complex body manipulations. Remember the poised, ready-to-attack position of the cats. You cannot effectively hit the ball unless both club and body are properly balanced.

Always take a long, long time moving the club away from the ball to the preparation position, calmly reversing the action toward the ball. This discipline eliminates stiff, jerky, and premature motion detrimental to timing. Body moves performed according to theory to which you cannot adjust will destroy the natural response to the club head so vital for long and accurate shots. *Always calmly prepare for impact, distance and accuracy.*

Fading, hooking remedies

Study position of the cats

Instinctive Hitting

6

You now understand the important fact that the ball is to be hit in one direction only; that the club is to be placed at the top of the backward motion for the purpose of striking the ball to the chosen target, and that to place the club at the top you must place it as calmly as possible so that you will be ready to reverse the action through the ball to the finish.

You also realize that when you take the club independently to the top, the body will remain balanced over the ball, ready and waiting to assist the club head in striking the ball. When performed naturally, the body will respond by coordinating with the club from the point of impact to the finish.

Body responds to performance

Many feel they should deliberately move their weight to the left through the use of their legs, get into a certain position, and then use the hands, arms, and club against the ball. This body shift or weight transference happens when the mind has focused upon striking the ball forward, to the left toward the target.

Bobby Jones made a good point about striking the ball. "When I hit it one way and it didn't do right, I'd try hitting it another way. I didn't try different swings. I probably didn't know there were such things, or even a swing at all for that matter.

"Golf is played by striking the ball with the head of the club. The objective of the player is not to swing the club in a specified manner, not to execute a series of complicated movements in a prescribed sequence, nor to look pretty while he is doing it, but primarily and essentially to strike the ball with the head of the club so that the ball will perform according to his wishes."*

Most important, you now have clearly in mind the fact that the whole purpose for the action is to hit the ball to the target. The importance of mental control and its effect upon action—whether during a friendly round or in competition—cannot be overemphasized.

Early in his career Ben Hogan learned about the importance of the proper mental approach.

"I soon found," he told *Golf World* magazine (December 7, 1971), "that only a few mental lapses cost me many strokes. I found I had to give my complete attention to every shot played from the drive to the short putt. After leaving the first tee, there could be no recess, no loafing spot on the mental side. You must feel in your mind that you are attacking the course, not the course attacking you. Whether you like the course or not, this is the course you must play."

A positive, aggressive approach to every shot also is important. Toward this end, Hogan added: "Make up your mind definitely on the club you need. Then play the club for all it's worth. Throw away any form of indecision. Forget any mistakes you may have made before playing the next shot. The most important shot

Marginal notes: Looking pretty not important

Marginal notes: On mental side stay alert

---

*From *Golf Is My Game,* copyright ©1959, 1960 by Robert Tyre Jones, Jr. and reprinted by permission of Doubleday and Company, Inc.

in golf is the one you have to play next.

"Don't take anything for granted, I mean especially the easy-looking shots. They can get you in more trouble than the tougher ones on which you know you have to concentrate. Never start a round with the feeling you have an alibi as an excuse. You must keep a firm grip on yourself—I mean on your mind and nerves. Make them work for you, not against you; keep them under control.

"Forget about self-pity when you get a bad lie or have a tough break; that is all part of the game. In golf, mind must be superior to matter, no matter what happens. Golf to me means to get an iron grip on the mental and nervous side, with the thought that I cannot afford to play even one careless stroke." **Bad breaks part of game**

So before you step up to the ball, survey the situation, decide upon the shot necessary and select the club which will provide the distance. Place the face of the club behind the ball to coincide with the line to the target and adjust your stance accordingly. Your body is balanced to this line, and you are ready to hit the ball. You never line your shoulders at the target and then adjust the club. You align the club first, then your body.

At this point you must be alert. Do you see accurately what must be done, and have you definitely decided what you want to accomplish? (Notice, I said "to accomplish." I did not refer to accomplishing the end result.) Are you retaining a singular purposeful thought? If so, you are ready to hit the ball. **Retain a purposeful thought**

I remember one golfer I was instructing. We came to a hole with an out-of-bounds on the left side of the fairway (a busy highway ran alongside the course). The clubhouse was situated to the right of the tee. When he addressed the ball he aimed at the clubhouse.

"Why are you aiming so far right?" I asked.

He pointed to the out-of-bounds. "Every time I step up to this tee, I feel I will hit the ball over the fence."

"Since you hit the ball out-of-bounds anyway," I said, "aim it out-of-bounds. I will give you a new ball if it goes out-of-bounds."

So he aimed slightly toward the fence and proceeded to hit the ball on to the fairway. I asked him why he did not hit the ball out-of-bounds.

Concentrate on your target

"I just couldn't allow myself to do it," he said.

You can see how the muscular system performs according to thought. You will see the traps, the lake, and other obstacles which affect your action—unless you decide to concentrate on sending the ball to the target. You hit the ball into the hazard because that is what you are thinking about.

When you stand on the tee or prepare to hit the second shot, your eyes automatically tell your brain the distance you desire the ball to travel to reach the green or the selected landing area on the fairway. From the tee, you see that a three wood is preferable. It would not only place you in better position, but would keep you out of trouble even if you hit the ball off line.

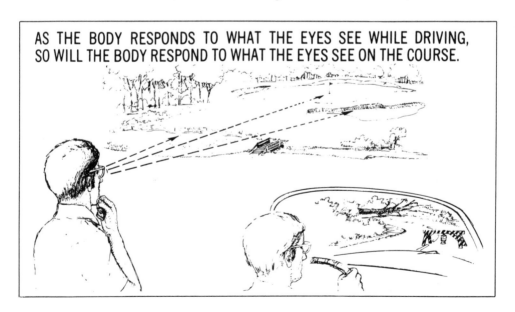

AS THE BODY RESPONDS TO WHAT THE EYES SEE WHILE DRIVING, SO WILL THE BODY RESPOND TO WHAT THE EYES SEE ON THE COURSE.

Whenever the eyes tell the brain you need not hit the ball with full action, they automatically tell it how much club-head impact is required to send the ball the distance they have seen. This needed impact automatically demands a given amount of backward motion. You do not have to calculate the amount of backward motion necessary; this is instinctive. Your God-given computer, your mind, will issue instructions for the correct coordination.

Use God-given computer

Your eyes also will tell you a slice is the shot to play. Or a hook. Or whether it is better to go over the trees, over the lake, or to hit the ball into the rough rather than onto the fairway for an easier entrance to the flag. Unless you pay attention to the messages the eyes transmit to the brain, you cannot hit the ball correctly.

Foundation for Hitting

Whether you must hit the ball over the trees, under the branches or against the wind, never conform your body movement to a predetermined formula or you will be unable to benefit from natural body response. Every shot played demands a body position relative to that shot. When this is assumed, you always feel balanced over the ball and for the target.

Try this experiment. Take the club to the top with your right hand and arm only. Keep your legs and feet inactive. Use the club as if to hit an imaginary ball. You will notice that as long as the body did not move around, the hand and arm were able to use the club well.

Experiment with right hand

Now place the club at the top again with a normal stance. Before moving the club head down toward an imaginary ball with the right hand, move the body toward the left ahead of the hand and arm. Notice you have a lifeless arm. The body pulls the arm dragging the hand, which in turn pulls the club at the imaginary

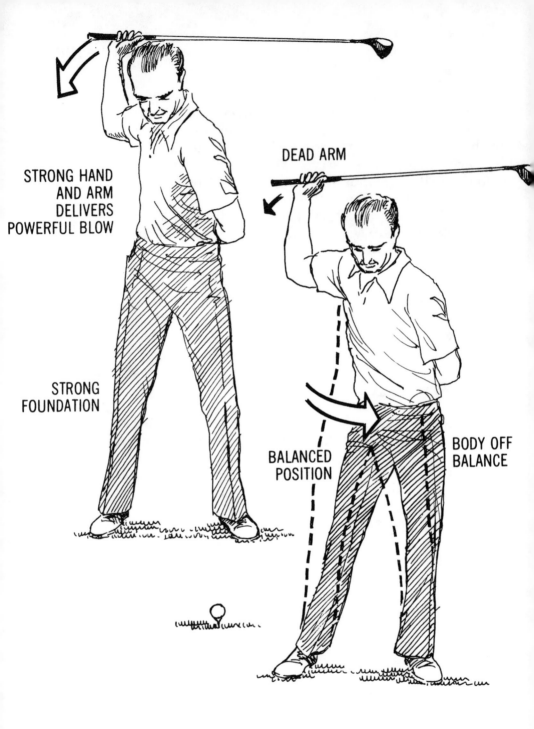

STRONG HAND
AND ARM
DELIVERS
POWERFUL BLOW

STRONG
FOUNDATION

DEAD ARM

BALANCED
POSITION

BODY OFF
BALANCE

ball. You cannot develop speed.

You will also notice that when the body moves, the arms cannot develop the circular centrifugal force to send the ball far, because they no longer have a foundation upon which to work. The arms, having a foundation upon which to move, can develop greater speed without losing accuracy.

Arms can develop speed

Now, I suggest you hit the ball without the use of your legs and feet. This will develop confidence that you can hit the ball far and accurately without consciously attempting to coordinate the various parts of your body. *When you have developed this confidence, allow your body to move instinctively and coordinate with the use of the club for a sudden impact.*

What is centrifugal force? It is an outward pull of the club away from its center (you) when in a circular motion. When your club reaches the bottom of the arc, where the ball is, it generates a pull away from you. When you sway or move around, there is no center for this force. A kick is a fine example of this force in action.

Outward pull in circular motion

One way to experience centrifugal force is by swinging the club while standing on a slippery floor. You will have to swing the club while you remain steady upon your feet. When you have learned to use the club upon this foundation, you will know how to use the club correctly. When in trouble imagine you are standing on ice and swing the club.

Your hands are the sole controlling factor using the club head to strike the ball. They initiate the movement of the club away from the ball, placing the club in the preparatory position, and return the club against the ball and into the finish. They work the club into a bent wrist position at the top without loosening the fingers around the shaft. No other portion of your body can precisely coordinate to thought or words as your hands.

Hands control club head

As your hands reach shoulder high at the top, they

bend at the wrist joint, positioning the club to be used against the ball. *While your attention is focused on the ball, your brain receives the message from your hands that they have the club poised for the same purpose—to hit the ball.* Practice mentally checking your hands. Are they coiled and in control of the club at this point before bringing the club against the ball? You will have to take a measure of time for this purpose. However, this is vital to timing and control. When the hands have positioned the club, your left arm should be allowed to bend somewhat. Not allowing the arm to flex will cause other portions of your body to become stiff as well, but more important, the relationship between your hands and your thought to calmly return the club toward the ball for flexible unleashing of the hands and club will be lost.

Allow left arm to bend

You will always hit the ball farther and more accurately when your left arm flexes at the top and continues in the flexed attitude until it reaches near the ball, at which time it receives a pull from the weight of the club, lengthens out, allows the wrists to snap or uncoil, sending the club against the ball with devastating force. The arm should bend immediately after impact, permitting the club head to continue unhindered into the finish. If your left arm becomes strong or stiff at this point, the action of the hands and club will be restricted.

Make a fist with left hand

Try another experiment. Make a fist with your left hand. Bend the arm placing the hand near the right shoulder. Move the hand downward toward an imaginary obstacle you desire to smash to the left. When the fist reaches this bottom position, allow the wrist to bend along with the left arm continuing into the finish above your left shoulder and to the left of your head. Force is applied in a circular manner, bending the left arm along with the wrist joint. Flexible force is applied when the hand and arm reach bottom.

ALLOW THE WRISTS
TO SNAP OR UNCOIL

TRY THIS
EXPERIMENT:
FLEXIBLE FORCE
IS APPLIED
WHEN THE HAND
AND ARM REACH
BOTTOM

109

Try a similar action with your right arm. Make a fist and bend the arm, placing the fist back of you in line with the right shoulder. Do not go above shoulder level. Bring the fist and arm downward toward the left in a circular motion of the forearm around the elbow. Apply the force in the same manner as the left when it reaches near bottom, toward the left and upward. The fist bends at the wrist joint along with the arm.

Fist bends at wrist joint

This exercise will strengthen the muscles necessary for golf. When you couple the action of the right and left using this thought, fluid action is developed through the ball, preventing hindering body movements and resisting tensions. *This cannot be attempted until you have eliminated unnecessary body contortions deemed necessary to generate a swing. A solid foundation will be required for these exercises.*

The perfect body alignment, timing the use of body weight, club-head snap against the ball, will be automatically achieved in this manner. It is imperative that you use your hands to initiate the club action and time its use. As they control the club at the top position, so should they control the club at the finish. In the finish, your hands should hold the club away from your body, head high, slightly to your left, with your body in an upright position facing the hole. You should never allow the hands to collapse their control immediately because you are finished or the ball has been hit.

Never allow hands to collapse

When your hands have control of the club in your finish, you will be sure they had control during impact. If your hands are not bent at the wrist joint in the finish, they will be stiff-wristed or dead during impact. Club-head action through the ball can be achieved only when the wrists bend with the motion of the club. When flexible action is restricted in the impact area, the club cannot move through the ball any faster than your stiff arm, shoulders, hips, legs, and other portions of your body can move.

You should restrict your body and use the club with your hands. This is to sense the motion of your club without unnecessary moves of your body. In hitting the ball, your body moves very little when moving the club away from the ball. While the hands reach the top, your body waits for the return of the club against the ball, ready to move with the club into the finish. You should never, never restrict or freeze your body at impact. It must move with the club, particularly from impact into the finish.

Body waits for club return

To further understand the control your hands have over the club for hitting, place your left toe on the ground about 15 inches behind your right foot. While in this balanced position, take the club with your hands and strike the ball. Your hands must bend at the wrist joints in order for you to retain balance. Your hands move the club to the top, return the club against the ball, and continue into the finish. This also is centrifugal force in action. When your arms or body attempts to generate the motion, you will find yourself unable to remain balanced. This is a fine way to learn how to control your club to hit the ball with maximum force and without losing balance.

WHILE IN THIS BALANCED POSITION, TAKE THE CLUB WITH YOUR HANDS AND STRIKE THE BALL.

Purpose and Timing

7

I do not know of a sport in which controlled thought, definite purpose, and a disciplined attitude are not needed. Golf is no exception. Every sport also requires a forward action toward your objective. In golf the action of the club head is for the purpose of sending the ball to a target—whether it be the fairway or the green. This is the reason I have mentioned in earlier chapters that placing the club back is really insignificant. It only prepares for the forward action.

For example, take several cardboard boxes and place them inside one another. A box will allow the club through and forward to the finish. Focus your attention against the side of the box. Take the club and hit the box. Use an old club for this purpose.

Cardboard box experiment

Observe that your attention and thought remained against the side of the box, not on the club moving away from the box to the top, or beginning its downward movement, or how you organized yourself in the process of hitting the box. The use of your hands

Body forms a foundation

and arms more than any other portions of the body becomes obvious. The body as a whole—the legs and feet—forms a foundation upon which to use the club and at the same time coordinate to the use of the club. Your move away from the box was without speed or strength. The purpose was to simply prepare to develop force at the point of contact. This force, generated instinctively at this point, caused the club to continue through the box into the finish.

There was no downward blow against the ground or floor—but against the box only. There never is a downward blow struck against the ball—only against the back of the ball as against the box.

Take long time to hit ball

A downward blow causes the weight of your body to remain on your right leg, keeping you behind the ball, stiffening the legs against the blow toward the ground, and forcing you to the right. The blow against the ball should take a long, long time. The desire to apply this force against the back of the ball toward the target will automatically move the body weight left, moving your legs left to balance this move. This is more a case of proper balance than a deliberate use of legs or knees.

Leg motion is always for the purpose of balancing for the use of force against an object you desire to propel to your left—the target. For example, a batter steps to balance himself to use the bat against a pitched ball; a boxer to punch a bag or opponent. Instinctively allowing the weight of the body to move into a balanced position to assist timing the club head against the ball

Allow balance of body weight

is the key. You will notice this takes place in every physical endeavor.

A downward blow will hit the ball against the ground and cause it to bounce off the turf without back spin of any consequence. All professionals take the turf (divot) in front of the ball toward the target, so the ball is hit cleanly—then the ground. Back spin is a result of the club face striking the bottom back of the ball before the club hits the turf. This proves that the club head approaches the ball with a forward angle rather than a downward blow.

The club chosen for the purpose of sending the ball to the target should not alter your decision to strike the back of the ball in the proper angle. Regardless of the length of the club, never change your purpose.

Now you can see the importance of your thought. The only thing left for you to do is to hit the ball with the force focused against the back of the ball as you did against the box. This will allow you to remain free during the entire action to synchronize and coordinate naturally as needed.

Synchronize naturally

Play such courses as Butler National Golf Club, Medinah Number Three, the Olympic Club, Winged Foot Golf Club, Augusta National Golf Club, The Dunes Golf and Beach Club, Cherry Hills Country Club or Oakmont Country Club, to name a few, and you will see why you must allow the body to respond to thought instinctively rather than to deliberately organize it to prevent hitting the ball into Robin Hood's forest, water, traps, or out-of-bounds. When confronted with such courses as these, you might instinctively tighten up. But if the body is allowed to perform without conscious observation or concern, you diminish this tension.

How to diminish tension

If the body is not capable of coordinating for the purpose which you decided upon, God made a mistake. And I would not dare to insult God by attempting to have you adjust, piece together, or consciously control movements which God has decreed must automatically respond to thought. So the forward thought must be maintained at all times. This must be focused upon the area which you desire the ball to reach.

Every individual, regardless of proficiency, is affected by thought. You see this every time you watch the touring professionals. Surely the weekend golfer should realize this fact as well. Your distractions are no greater or less than the professional's. Only the type of competition differs. The pressure is the same. Though you may disregard this fact, it is nevertheless true, as you will note particularly when you step up to the first tee.

Why should people standing around that first tee cause your muscle memory to disappear?

Yet how different it is after you have left the first tee and settled down to the feeling of hitting the ball the way you know you can hit it. When you focus properly, you hit the ball correctly. When fear to any degree manifests itself, the coordination essential to fine golf disappears. Distance becomes blurred, indecision causes trouble, and spastic reactions become the rule.

Proper focus; correct hit

Carl Tash is a fine example of how the mind can control even a difficult situation. Carl was involved in a near-fatal automobile accident on July 6, 1975. An operation fused the bones in his neck and spine, limiting most of his turning ability from the shoulders.

Prior to this accident, Carl had learned how to adjust his coordination to the use of the club in the full movement I have described. After recuperation, he had to adjust the use of the club to a limited movement of the body. Through a calm, focused attention on the use of the club, placing it back to a certain level only, then allowing the body to automatically adjust to the use of the club through impact into the finish, Carl is able to play competitive golf on a collegiate level. His back swing is very short, but he plays a fine game of golf.

Short back swing, but fine game

"Until the near-fatal car accident that I suffered," Carl says, "I was a very confident golfer who felt a real love for the game. This feeling I attribute to you. After the car accident, and spinal fusion of the neck (that removed most of the turning ability of my shoulders), I thought my dream of being able to play competitive golf had ended. But your great reputation for teaching the young and handicapped was proven to be all that people said it was . . . and more!

"After the operation, you were still able to develop for me a swing that once again gives me the confidence and playing ability to become a successful, competitive golfer. I have yet to meet a professional who can match your very simple, yet successful, teaching methods. This new swing that you have given me, once again, has brought much enjoyment to my golf and life."

Then there is Bruce A. Clinton, a Ph.D. research scientist with Searle Laboratories. Due to a service-connected injury which involved the permanent loss of innervation and 75 percent loss of the use of the left *latissimus dorsi,* as well as rib damage, Clinton has developed a golf action suited to him.

Handicapped; sound game

"Despite the trauma of this accident, I have developed a relatively sound game, thanks to your method," he wrote me. "It is still improving, but my swing is near normal, which includes a full torsion of the shoulders. Although my swing is best suited for me, and may not be appropriate for another golfer, I am comfortable and under no strain due to the stretch at the back of my swing."

Both of these individuals have been able to develop a unique method of hitting the ball as a result of focusing attention upon calmly placing the club and then hitting right at the ball to the finish.

Sudden Impact and Timing

How do you develop this sudden impact, this tremendous striking force? By achieving a flexible, resilient action in your swing. To attain proper muscular response, avoid thinking about the positioning of the muscles during the action of the club.

Keep swing flexible

To develop a sudden impact, you must be balanced at all times. You must keep your hands flexible at the wrist joints so they can bend at will. You cannot generate greater force by gripping the club tightly. The tighter you hold the club, the slower the club head moves. Although you remain flexible, your fingers

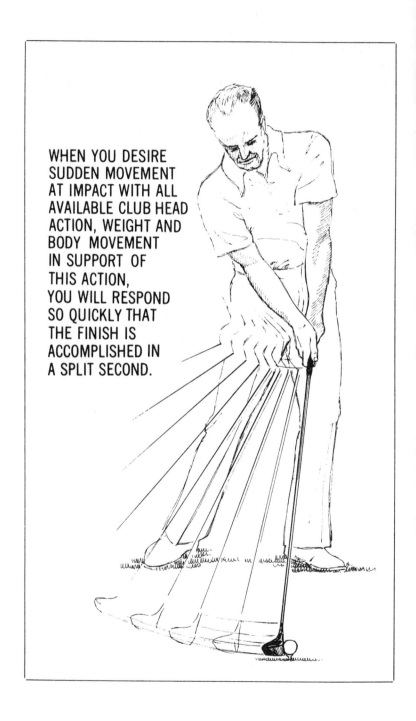

WHEN YOU DESIRE
SUDDEN MOVEMENT
AT IMPACT WITH ALL
AVAILABLE CLUB HEAD
ACTION, WEIGHT AND
BODY MOVEMENT
IN SUPPORT OF
THIS ACTION,
YOU WILL RESPOND
SO QUICKLY THAT
THE FINISH IS
ACCOMPLISHED IN
A SPLIT SECOND.

never let go of the club. This is important.

When you desire sudden movement at impact with all available club head action, weight and body movement in support of this action, you will respond so quickly that the finish is accomplished in a split second. You will never know how this was performed. However, it will always be your individual manner and coordination which accomplishes this action. When you have a sudden mental awareness of the job at hand, and come alive mentally for a purpose, your body will respond in a well-coordinated effort through the ball into the finish.

Body responds to awareness

This mental attitude should never weaken in its determination to send the ball to the target. However, one cannot maintain this fixed purpose when the mind is focused upon mechanical excellence or positional moves. There is no such thing as muscular or mechanical memory. Muscle memory is the result of a purposeful thought projected each time you approach the ball. If muscle memory were a fact, you could think of numerous other things, ignore sound, or worry about the outcome of a shot when ready to hit the ball. Yet you see the finest of players move away from a shot because of disturbing sounds or indecision as to how to best play the shot. A constant, repeated thought facilitates timing and repeated muscular response.

How do you achieve this timing? By proper use of words.

Thought affects timing

The word *swing* refers to a number of actions—from the ball, back to the ball, into the finish. However, such words as *boom, bang,* and *hit* have more limited meaning. The words *strike* and *snap* demand a like response.

Thus from the moment you take the club in your hands, approach the ball for address, and line it up for the target, do so with a mind determined to hit, bang, snap, etc. for a lightning attack of the club head against

119

the ball. One way to implement this kind of action is to say to yourself, *"C-a-l-m-l-y, hit the ball."*

Notice how the word *calmly* is spaced out to conform to a calm attitude of placing the club to the top, ready to return the club for the purpose of hitting the ball, while the word *hit* is sharp and short. Using the club simultaneously with the words will produce a timed action.

Using words produces action

A Karate demonstration proves the effectiveness of the use of these words. Attention never leaves the object upon which force is to be applied. You make a sound at the same time force is applied against the object. This vocal expression increases unified motion for greater strength. Effort is not wasted while moving away or toward the object.

Use the club similarly in golf: Focus your mind on the force of the club head against the ball. This stimulates flexible effort from the body at this point.

Important: Did you use the club at the same time as you uttered the words, after the words, or before uttering the words? When the club is used at the *same time* you will experience an overall, well coordinated action. It will be *powerful in application,* and *facilitates perfect timing.*

There will be no conscious control over the muscular system. Your attention will not be diverted from the address to the arms, legs, knees, feet, shoulders, or on shifting weight or countless other distractions which destroy coordination. The body is always allowed to synchronize with the club action, led by the hands and arms. The position and muscular alignment of your body will be perfect, according to your physical ability.

Keep attention on address

The way you hit the ball with the club head will determine the flight of the ball. You cannot control the flight once the ball has been hit. Therefore, your primary and most important concern should be the simple and singular goal of hitting the ball.

Fear of a bad shot is one of the greatest concerns a golfer faces. To offset this fear you must focus your attention completely, determinedly, and resolutely on the purpose for the club in your hand.

When watching touring professionals, you will notice a difference in action away from the ball and toward the ball, but they all look very much alike at impact. This is the crucial area of golf. Many look alike at the finish as well.

Impact is crucial area

When your hands control the club toward impact, the arms lead moving the body into a balance. As the shoulders move, the hips and legs also move into a sound foundation. Perfect hitting position and balance are achieved. Your body will be as properly organized at the ball as that of the best players.

Two-Point Control

An exercise which will aid you in controlling the club and the coordination of the body is what I call a "two-point control." This involves placing the club in a suitable position on the backward motion—a position conducive to striking the ball accurately. Then reverse the action and place the club in a finish position while retaining balance. Do not think of speed or impact at this time. Practice placing the club back no higher than your shoulder, then place the club *instantly* in the finish. This will help you develop one forward movement to impact and into the finish without positional interference in between. This is not as easy as you may think. However, it is mental training which counts. The body instantly responds in like manner in a unified action.

Place club at shoulder level

Placing the club too far back, too high above your shoulders, around in back of you or in front of you will cause difficulty in bringing the club instantly into a balanced finish. Therefore, by practicing the

121

placement method you will find the position which will allow a coordinated move into the finish.

When you find the proper position, you will suddenly feel the club weight act at the bottom and finish in a certain balance peculiar to you. You have time then to reverse your action and thought when you place the club back. Take time to be ready to reverse the action to hit the ball. There is no need to speed the club downward toward the ball.

No need
to speed club

At first you may think you have placed your club in a certain position, when instead you have wandered from one position to another. You must come to a definite stop in placing the club; the same in the finish. You must come to a definite place where you feel comfortable and in a balanced position. Make your moves positive. Such discipline will increase your enjoyment of the game because the ball will respond correctly and your score will be better.

When you fall away from these disciplines, listen to inexpert advice, attempt mechanical control, etc., you will become confused.

You cannot go wrong when you place the club on the backward movement no higher than the shoulders at any time, and into a higher position in the finish. You always place the club lower in the back movement than into the finish. Practice from three-quarters of the way back into a higher finish.

Practice
higher finish

When placing the club into the finish, your body should be straight, with the hands holding the club high. Placing the club is always done with the hands. The hands and the mind should always coordinate perfectly.

Practicing this thought and action will give you a personal action—not one which fits Trevino, Nicklaus, Snead, Hogan, Palmer, Patty Berg, Carol Mann or others who play fine golf.

Your body weight, muscular strength, and balance in

122

motion will automatically help send the ball. This is the only way confidence is developed, not through deliberate mechanical control.

A change in thought causes a change in muscular response. We are not muscle alone. The entire body response is controlled by the mind. This is God's law. Missed shots, indecision, bad breaks, cause the golfer to examine the cause for error and begin experimenting. A muscular change is the result. Ben Hogan, superb in mechanical movements, found it necessary to discipline himself mentally to become a champion. Others equally great also found this to be true.

Find cause for error

Their secret, your secret, is disciplined thought. With little room available, you can hold a club down to the metal shaft and allow your physical response to follow your thought of using the club. Picture the results you desire. Hit the ball the simplest way possible to you.

Perfect Finish

A balanced finish is important. The finish is a result of natural response to motion, not to consciously controlled mechanical moves.

The "two-point control" is designed to synchronize the action of the club and body. The "sudden impact," "calm-hit," "boom," "bang," or "hit" exercise is designed to develop controlled effort in one area. This effort must never be performed with strong or stiff muscular effort. It should not be against a stiff left side. It must be an effort of the club head and the body in motion. Emphasis of greater activity of club head against the ball is focused in this area. This club head activity will demand natural body response for continued coordination through the ball into the finish.

Sudden impact helps control

When you prepare yourself for force in this area, with the understanding that you must continue to respond to the pull of that force, motion will not be impeded and

Purpose and Timing

THE
BALANCED
FINISH

a synchronized coordinated body action will result in a balanced finish. When you desire the club to strike the ball to a given target, a body response adjusts to this desire and moves with the force of the club through the ball to a finish.

The degree of motion and the height of your finish will depend upon the amount of force or effort needed at impact to send the ball a given distance. This effort or force of impact against the ball will develop a pull of the club head through the ball, demanding coordination from the body and stopping in a position past the ball upon diminished speed of the club head. You never have to calculate the amount of follow-through necessary for any given shot. Tremendous force at impact results in a high finish, medium force a lower finish and so on down to the chip shot which requires very little finish.

Impact force
develops pull

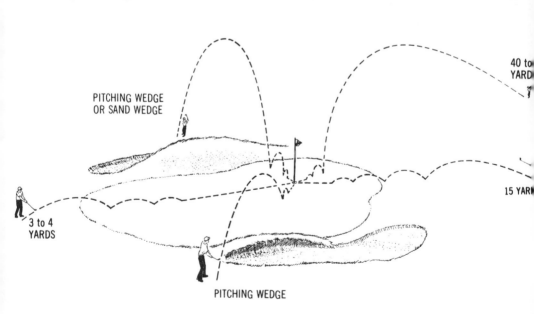

PITCHING WEDGE
OR SAND WEDGE

40 to
YARD

15 YAR

3 to 4
YARDS

PITCHING WEDGE

Stroke Savers

8

After dubbing a number of shots, you find yourself about 100 yards from the green. Can a shot be saved at this point? Absolutely. Always attempt to play your best regardless of the circumstances. Accuracy from 100 yards into the green is of the utmost importance. In order to play the shot accurately, you must develop a confident, aggressive attitude. This kind of attitude comes by constant practice.

Practice brings confident attitude

The Full Short Iron
For most, 100 yards may be a full shot into the green. The stance and body balance will be somewhat different from other shots. The feet, for this and all short shots, should be placed in what is known as an open stance. An open stance is merely the best-balanced position for the shot. Draw a line from the ball to your target. Draw a parallel line for your feet. The distance will be determined by the short iron selected. Place your

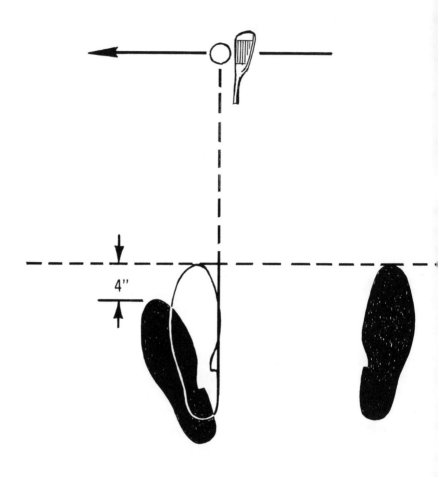

toes against this line. Turn your left foot left and pull it back about four inches. This will turn your body more toward the target. All short shots should have this body balance. The exact placement of your left foot away from the line must be determined by your physical build and feeling of balance. Your right toe may or may not point at this line.

Facing toward the target rather than the ball helps you hit the ball in that direction easily. Your weight will be more on the left leg.

Rik Massengale, one of golf's top touring professionals (left) calls Gus Bernardoni's way "a new and interesting approach to the game of golf—an interesting look into the mental as well as the physical side of playing golf." (Photo courtesy of John E. Olson.)

Bernardoni (2nd from right) plays a round with former Chicago Bear gridders Virgil Carter (left) and the late Brian Piccolo (right), along with Adolph Bertucci, greens superintendent at the Lake Shore Country Club in Glencoe, Ill.

Despite a fractured spine incurred as a World War II paratrooper, Gus Bernardoni became an excellent golfer under the tutelage of such experts as Manuel de la Torre, presently head professional, Milwaukee Country Club, Milwaukee, Wisc. (Photo courtesy of The Chicago Tribune.)

(below) Viet Nam veteran Marine Corps PFC Paul D. Allen practices for the Grove School for Handicapped Children benefit tournament under the watchful eye of Chicago pros Hubby Habjan, Gus Bernardoni and Bob Harris, while fellow veteran and Great Lakes Naval Hospital patient PFC David A. Stokes waits his turn.

RADM Howard A. Yeager (left), 9ND commandant, shows his trophy collection to pros Hubby Habjan, Bob Harris and Gus Bernardoni before they tee off in benefit tournament for Grove School for Handicapped Children.

Handicapped golfers George Becker (left) and John McGough have been helped to highly respectable scores by Gus Bernardoni. Becker lost his arm at the age of 8; McGough has no radius in his right arm.

Touring pro Lynn Lott (left) and Bernardoni. (Photo courtesy of John E. Olson.)

Host Pat Robertson of CBN's "700 Club" (left) learns from guest Gus Bernardoni. Inside the 700 Club studio, Bernardoni joins co-hosts and singer by the clock (right).

Sandra Clifford Fullmer, winner of many international amateur tournaments, including the Mexican, German and Spanish opens.

Audrey Spak now plays pain-free golf in spite of spinal disease, thanks to help from Bernardoni (see Chapter 13).

(below) Golfers line up for Dixie Classic Pro-Am tournament in Jacksonville, Fla.

Bernardoni (left) receives winner's trophy after 3-stroke margin victory in Illinois PGA Senior Champion-ship, 1974, with 144 score. Trophy presented by Steve Blatnak, professional, Ridgemoor Country Club, Chicago, Ill.

These sequence photos reve smooth swing of Pro Gus Berna doni. (Photos courtesy of Lou Carter, Jr., Professional, Hillcre Country Club, Long Grove, Ill.)

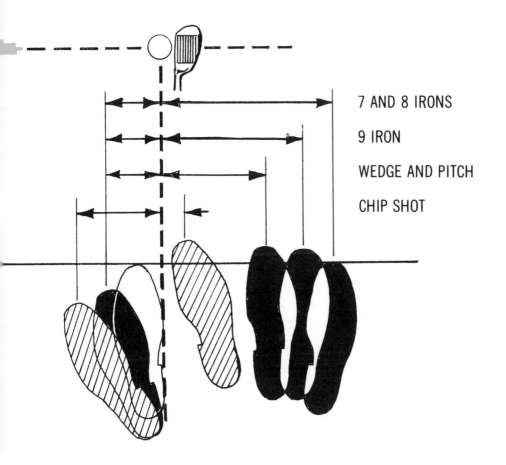

7 AND 8 IRONS

9 IRON

WEDGE AND PITCH

CHIP SHOT

Pitch Shot

When the ball is flown onto the green from any distance, it is considered a pitch shot. Your stance for the shot will depend upon the club used. The club used will demand that you bend from the waist to accommodate its length, restricting the use of the club away from the ball. The more your body bends from the waist, the less freedom you have for a large action away from the ball. Your action should always be greater and more forceful through the ball. Your desire to hit the ball a given dis-

PITCH SHOT:
THE CLUB USED WILL
DEMAND THAT YOU
BEND FROM THE WAIST
TO ACCOMMODATE
ITS LENGTH

tance, and this body restriction against moving the club away from the ball, automatically controls the amount of backward motion necessary for the shot. Never move beyond this point of restriction or you will have to move off the ball, sway, or make other moves that destroy accuracy.

Make sure your hands and arms have the room to move past your body without hindrance. It is imperative that you stop bending your body when the club touches the ground.

The club selected for this shot depends upon where the flag is positioned on the green. If the flag is placed in a corner or back portion of the green, you may desire to use an eight or nine iron. Many use a wedge regardless. If the flag is on the front edge of the green or tucked behind a trap, you must use your wedge or possibly your sand wedge for greater loft, as you try to drop the ball dead at the flag. If you are doubtful, play the center of the green.

Use wedge for loft

Score-saving shots are within this range. You must stop the ball quickly in order to prevent it from bouncing into the tall grass, trap or lake. Hitting the ball sharply and cleanly, before the club takes turf, imparts backspin. Practice stopping the ball quickly without taking turf. A *sharp* forward motion of the club head against the bottom back portion of the ball will produce

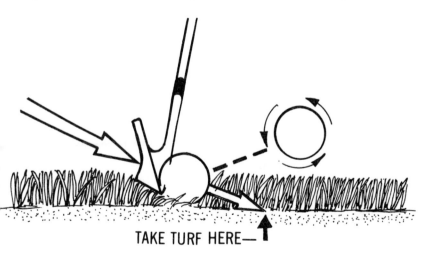

TAKE TURF HERE—

THE BALL WILL STOP RAPIDLY

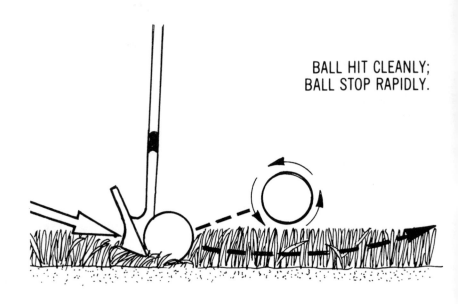

BALL HIT CLEANLY;
BALL STOP RAPIDLY.

this backspin. This action must be used for all shots, particularly when playing to the green.

The ball is placed off the left heel on all shots. Never place the ball in the center or back of center unless absolutely necessary. As a result of this placement, you will strike the ball and take turf in front of the ball as professionals do. Placing the ball at center or back of center may cause you to hit the top of the ball or press the ball against the turf, making it bounce off the ground and result in a flyer.

Ball placement critical

Although you feel your weight on your left, it is balanced on both feet. All positions assumed over the ball must be for the purpose of striking the ball to the flag. If the ball is back of center, your weight will also be to the right rather than toward the left. With the weight on the right, it is difficult to coordinate with the club toward the target.

HIT DOWN—BALL BOUNCES
OFF TURF, ROLLS UPON LANDING

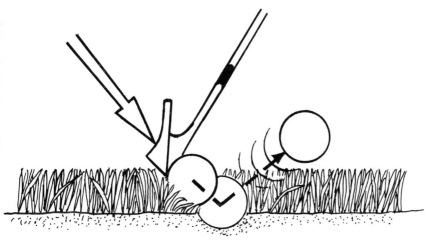

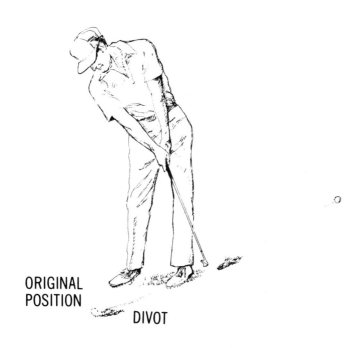

ORIGINAL
POSITION

DIVOT

Your follow-through for short shots is a result of the amount of impact—hit—required to send the ball a given distance. When the club is used for a sudden, flexible impact at the ball, the follow-through will finish higher than expected. Remember, if your club speed is downward, or you hit with force downward, the club more than likely will stop as you strike the ball, or shortly thereafter. A follow-through is difficult. You will have to force yourself into the finish.

CHIP   PITCH AND RUN

ALL FINISHES DEPEND
UPON AMOUNT OF FORCE
AGAINST THE BALL.

PITCH SHOT

FULL WEDGE

Pitch and Run

This shot can be played when the ground between you and the green does not hinder the ball from bouncing toward the green. Your decision to land the ball well short of the green, near the green or on the fringe of the green will depend upon the surface condition and the placement of the flag.

In order to play this shot, you must determine how far to carry the ball and how much roll is needed to reach the flag. A six, seven or eight iron may be used. Although many desire to play this shot in preference to the pitch shot, I recommend that you fly the ball to the surface of the green whenever possible. This eliminates the possibility of having the ball bounce into trouble.

However, never discount the pitch-and-run shot when applicable.

Your stance and ball placement are the same as for other shots. Your right foot will move toward the left, narrowing the stance somewhat. Narrowing your stance will depend upon your physical characteristics.

Applying an aggressive attitude, strike the ball with a clean, sharp action of the club head. This controls the bounce and roll of the ball upon landing. Never allow worry over mechanical positioning, amount of backswing, or possible end results to destroy your ability to execute this shot. Once a decision has been reached, allow your computer—mind—to demand response from your body.

Keep worry under control

This shot will be executed mostly with your hands and arms. Holding your club shorter will give you greater control. This progressive shortening of your club depends upon the distance of the shot. The less length in your hands, the more control you exert over the shot; the higher your hands are on the club, the greater your difficulty in handling the length of the club. Your body will remain more passive, acting as a balanced foundation for your hands and arms. Using your hands and arms more than your body will increase your accuracy.

Chipping

To successfully play a chip shot, you should place your feet close together and use your hands a great deal. Placing the ball off your left heel, balance your weight on both feet while leaning slightly left. This increases your feel for the hole.

Balance weight on both feet

Regardless of the short distance the ball travels to reach the green, you must strike the ball sharply in order to have good control of its forward motion. The ball will lay down quickly and roll nicely to the hole. Practice this sharp impact until you learn how much

action is necessary. Remember, hold the club as short as possible. Your hands, moving simultaneously to your thought, control this sharp action. When your thought is calm and without anxiety over the swing from the ball and back towards the ball, you can control the club for accuracy. You can then think: "I will take the club and strike the ball there (to the flag)." If you decide to lob the ball to the green, your hands will take the club and move to this thought, producing the shot desired. Regardless of the shot, your hands automatically adjust to your thought and produce the necessary action of the club.

Hands adjust to thought

Simply remain quiet and strike the ball to the hole. Practice until you gain confidence that all you need to do is to hit the ball to the flag with the head of the club. Continue this attitude until you master the free, uncomplicated use of the club. No one can feel the club in your fingers as you can feel it. No one sees the shot as your eyes see it. No one can sense your apprehension over this shot as you. Become a free agent. Play the game using your own talents as best you can. No one can exert control over yourself as you can.

Conscious control over mechanical movements is a sure road to failure. Worry over technique, outcome of the shot, or the pressure to get it close, causes failure. All these are negatives. Discipline in this area of play is vital. Maintain a disciplined positive, aggressive attitude. Give yourself the benefit of the doubt. It matters not that you play this shot differently than someone else; successful results are what count. Play your game with the coordination God gave you, instead of trying to imitate someone else.

Avoid negatives

Placement of the flag will determine the club necessary for the shot. The distance the ball must travel to clear the longer grass is important. One look from the ball to the green, from the edge of the green to the hole, will determine the club and force needed to reach the hole. The grass between you and the green usually is not very long. When the flag is close, use a lofted club. When the flag is well back on the green, use a less lofted club, landing the ball on the green near you and rolling the remainder of the distance. You will be more accurate when rolling the ball than lofting the ball to the flag.

When on the fringe, you can use the putter with greater success. To learn which club to use for the short shots, use common sense. Hold a ball in your hand. Look to see whether you should lob the ball high and far, or short and not so high, or simply roll the ball to the hole. This will give you an idea of which lofted club is needed for the shot. Remember, when near the green you will have greater success rolling the ball to the hole than lofting the ball. When lofting a chip to the flag, make certain there is not a hard area that would bounce the ball over the green, or soft area to stop the ball short.

Use putter on fringe

To learn the impact necessary to send the ball a given distance, ignore all slopes between the ball and hole. Strike the ball sharply from different distances. It is the

YOU WILL BE AMAZED HOW LITTLE FORCE IS NEEDED TO ROLL THE BALL THE NECESSARY DISTANCE.

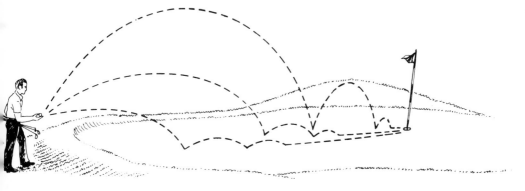

impact which sends the ball to the hole and not the effect of your backswing. You will be amazed how little force will be needed to roll the ball the necessary distance. This small motion improves control and accuracy. Learn to strike the ball for distance before trying to compensate for slopes.

When wedge
is proper club

When the ball is snuggled in deep grass or lands behind a trap, your pitching wedge or sand wedge will be the proper club to use. Experiment with these clubs for saving many an errant shot. When faced with a fast green, your pitching wedge would be safer to use. A fast downhill green can best be played by using a putter when very close to the putting surface. If the grass is short between you and the ball, your putter is still the best choice. In all circumstances, use common sense rather than prescribed techniques. From the full shot to the chip, your hands control the club.

Pressure the
Ball Out

9

Missing the green and ending in the sand trap need not be disaster. Learning how to play the trap shot will not only get you back on the green, but also will build confidence in your ability to extricate yourself from other trouble in the game. Thus learning to play the trap shots is more important than just getting back on the green.

All shots demand control of the club. The control of the club in this situation is still in the fingers. The hands are really critical here. You will learn that a sound foundation is extremely important when playing trap shots. The less you use your body in this action, the greater your accuracy.

Club control in fingers

All sand shots demand a strong footing. You must always work your feet well into the sand. Not only is this necessary for a sound foundation, but it provides a method for judging the condition of the sand. You must determine whether the sand is soft and fluffy, soft only a few inches and then packed, coarse and heavy, packed from rain, or shallow with hard ground immediately under the surface.

Now let's assume you're in the sand. What's the difference between the sand wedge and the pitching wedge?

Holding the wedges at the neck with the grip pointing at the ground, look at the sole of each club. (This is the part of the head that rests on the ground when the club is held by the handle.) You will notice the difference between the leading edge and the back edge of the club. On the pitching wedge the leading edge is higher than the back edge. This is so the club will not bounce when it hits the ground but will catch the ground and dig into the turf. The sand wedge has a hump near the back portion of the sole which will allow the club to slide through the sand. The leading edge is lower than this hump and will not catch the sand, which would dissipate the force of the swing. This is the major difference. The other difference is the weight of

When club rests on ground

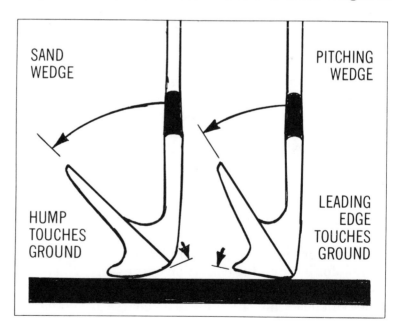

144

the two clubs. The sand wedge is heavier. The length is the same.

The sand wedge also can be used in long, heavy grass, when the ball has to be lofted high and dropped dead upon the green. This club is particularly good when there is a small tree between you and the green and when the pitching wedge might not abruptly loft the ball.

Now, how do you use the club?

Place the ball on hard ground where there is little grass. Make a line to some target from the ball and place the ball on this line. Now place the club behind the ball as you would in the sand, with the hump on the ground while the leading edge is off the ground. You will notice that the face of the club is practically toward the sky. The club wobbles when the hump is placed upon the hard surface. (Were you to place the pitching wedge next to this club, you would find that club sitting absolutely flat on the ground). The face will

Place ball
on hard ground

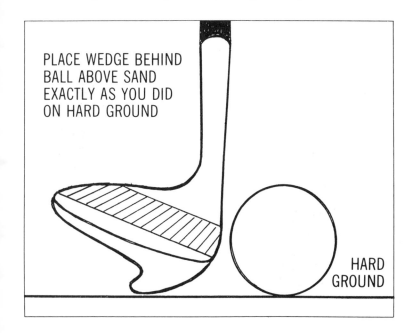

PLACE WEDGE BEHIND
BALL ABOVE SAND
EXACTLY AS YOU DID
ON HARD GROUND

HARD
GROUND

aim toward the right. Take the club and strike the hump against the ground. Notice how it bounced. Hitting the hump into the sand will allow the club to glide through it.

In order to have the club face square to the line of flight you will have to face more to the left when you hold the club correctly. This will be noticeable when

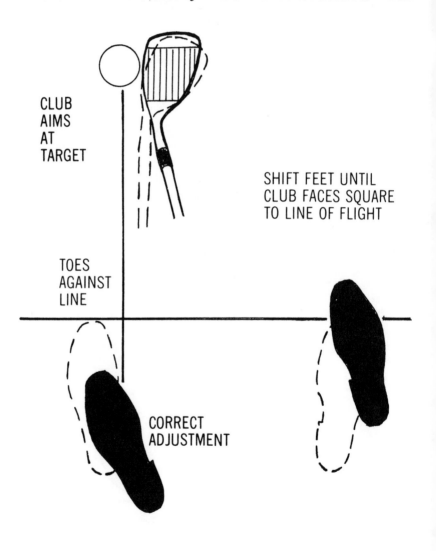

CLUB AIMS AT TARGET

SHIFT FEET UNTIL CLUB FACES SQUARE TO LINE OF FLIGHT

TOES AGAINST LINE

CORRECT ADJUSTMENT

you draw another line parallel to the line of flight for your feet. You should always hold the club with the face more open than normal so you can get elevation quickly. Your feet will then point more to the left of the line of flight.

To learn this stance, place your toes against the line. Shift your feet left until the club face is square to the line of flight. Your left side will pull away from the line while the right moves over the line. This is known as an open stance. When it is assumed, the club face will aim at your target.

Three Sand Shots

The perfect lie is when the ball sits beautifully on top of the sand. Another sand shot is used when the ball has hit dry sand and has forced it away from the ball, so that the ball is almost below the surface of the sand. (This is known as the "fried egg.") Still another type of shot is used when the sand is wet and the ball lands in the sand but remains in its own mark. This is known as the "plugged ball." Then there are lies in which the ball does not quite make it through the sand and stops on the up-slope near the edge of the green—or the opposite situation when it lands on the downward slope near the rear edge of the trap.

Let's consider the shot in which the ball is sitting nicely on top of the soft, fluffy sand. Remember to have the hump of the club near the sand rather than the leading edge. When you hit the hard ground with the hump, you notice that the club bounces. Without a ball, place the hump of the club on the sand and notice the wide mark the hump leaves. Imagining yourself playing a regular sand shot, take the club and hit this hump against the sand. Notice how the club glides through the sand.

Practice this hitting of the hump against the sand until you feel how easy it is to force the sand in front of the

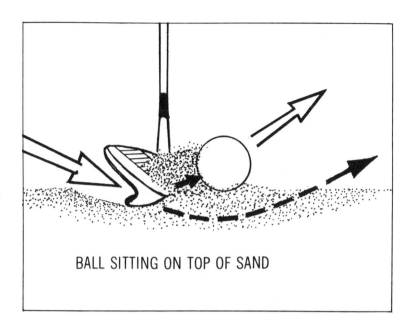

BALL SITTING ON TOP OF SAND

club, building sand pressure between the ball and the club, forcing the ball out and onto the green. Make a long, semi-lazy motion hitting the club sharply at the sand. In the sand your action away from the ball can be big, though your finish should vary according to the force necessary to send the ball a given distance. Never strike the sand with the leading edge or the club will be drawn deeply into the sand and act like a plow.

Now work your feet deep into the sand. Not only does this provide a sound balance, but it will tell you whether the sand is soft from the surface to the bottom, or from the surface to a short distance under the surface. This information is important to determine the type of sand blast required to extricate the ball.

Work feet
deep into sand

The ball should be placed in line with the left heel or possibly a bit in front of it. This can be determined only from experience. The ball should not be played off the right foot unless absolutely necessary because of the terrain or because of a plugged ball. Bend from the waist sufficiently to hold the club just off the sand. Remember, according to USGA Rules of Golf, you cannot touch the sand with the club or any portion of the club in advance of the shot. It will cost you a penalty. So you bend over just enough to hold the club comfortably above the sand, with the hands and arms away from the body so that they will not be hampered.

Angle of club face determines flight.

Your hands hold the club as in all other shots, though the face may be turned more open. Now you will be facing more left than the flight of the ball. Facing the ball too much forces you to close the face or hit the ball to the right. On the other hand, facing the target more than necessary hinders the motion away from the ball and coordination at impact.

Remember, the sand is what sends the ball to the green—not the club itself. The club hits the sand with sufficient force so the build-up of sand between the club face and the ball actually does the job. Your hands pick the club up more abruptly. Keep your body constant, using the upper portion more than legs, hips and feet. Your upper body is the major coordinating portion in all shots, but particularly in the sand shot. Facing left, the club face will not strike on a line to the flag but on a line left of the target. This keeps the face open, lofting the ball out of the sand.

Practice hitting sand

How hard should you hit the sand to send the ball a given distance? This can be learned only through practice. The texture of sand may be different from course to course, and this will affect the amount of force used. A full finish is not always required. When near the green, you may make a bigger movement away from the ball than for a pitch-and-run or chip shot, but finish shortly after hitting the sand. Don't cut your backward motion short.

Now let's discuss the "fried egg." Here the ball has sunk deeply into the sand so all you can see is its top. When the sand is soft, the force of the ball pushes the

150

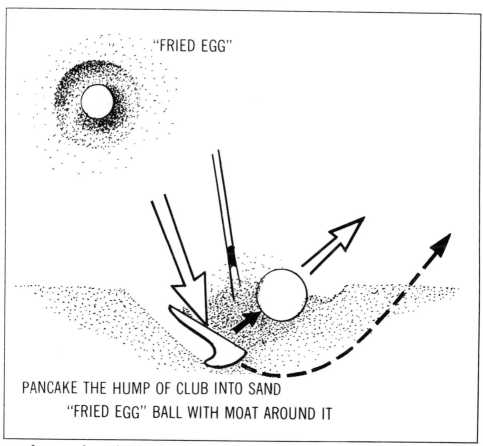

"FRIED EGG"

PANCAKE THE HUMP OF CLUB INTO SAND
"FRIED EGG" BALL WITH MOAT AROUND IT

sand away from it giving the appearance of a fried egg. There is always a moat around the ball when the sand is soft and fluffy. On the downstroke bang the hump deeply into the sand to get under the ball so the sand can force the ball out. When the sand is not soft and fluffy, you will need to close the face slightly and hit downward so the club can get low enough, forcing the sand to push the ball out. When the club has to be closed somewhat, you will need to place the ball off the right foot or near the right foot. Depending upon the texture of the sand, you may have to face the ball more than the standard shot.

How do you play a plugged ball, lying in its indentation in wet sand? The ball is played well behind the right foot. Your feet will be in a square position. You must close the face of the club again, placing the leading edge so the sand will catch the club and draw the club deeply into the sand.

Playing a plugged ball

You will need a downward blow which will send the club sufficiently below the ball. To accomplish this downward blow, pick the club straight up and chop down forcefully with the leading edge. Allow the club to sink deeply into the sand well below the ball and plow forward. There should be no deliberate attempt to follow through because you are hitting into packed, wet sand. However, the force applied will continue through and into a finish. This shot will cause the ball to fly lower and run faster upon landing on the green. Therefore you must take into account the fact that it

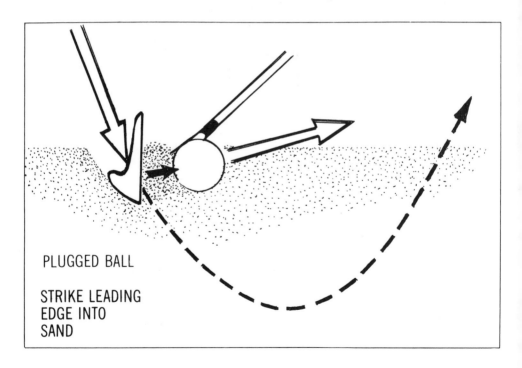

PLUGGED BALL

STRIKE LEADING
EDGE INTO
SAND

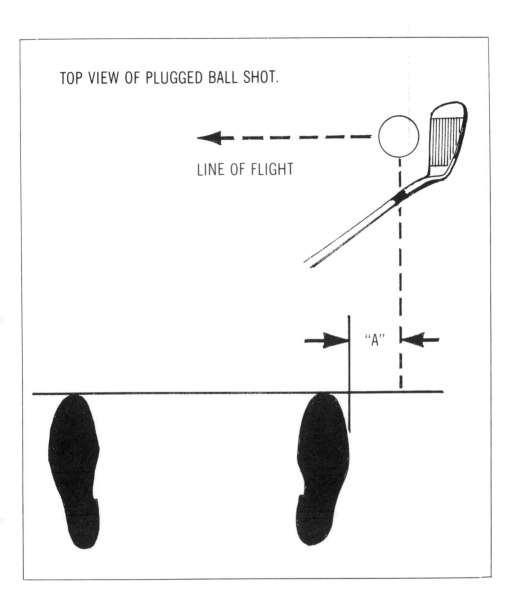

TOP VIEW OF PLUGGED BALL SHOT.

LINE OF FLIGHT

"A"

will run. Whatever you do, get the ball out—even if you
have a long putt coming back. This shot requires you to
take the club straight up and straight down into the
sand behind the ball.

Upward or Downward Slopes

When the ball does not get through the sand but stops on the up-slope near the green, it presents a tough shot. You will have the ball above your feet and you will be standing with one leg above the other in order to make the shot. You will have to consider carefully the amount of slope confronting you. Perhaps you could chip the ball with better results. However, when you blast make certain the club is wide open.

Hit sand
in upward blow

You must face considerably left of target. Hit the sand in an upward blow as you cut under the ball. The ball will fly high, but at least you should be on the green. You must exert more force than usual. Many times you can use the club normally against the sand as well as up the slope. If the ball is buried, you should slam the club against the slope as well as up the slope with enough force to push the sand against the ball, forcing it upward and out.

Hit sand with
downward
blow

When the slope is downward and the ball is sitting on top of the sand on the far side of the trap, you will also have a difficult shot. Here you will need to bring the club downward into the sand and keep the face sufficiently open to loft the ball to the green. Practice pancaking the hump of your club hard against the sand, placing the club deep and under the ball and forcing the sand against the ball.

Hitting from Outside the Trap

You are faced with making a shot in which the ball is in the trap, but you must stand outside the trap. This position will require you to bend over considerably more to allow the club to strike the sand. This takes

Delicate balance
outside trap

delicate balance. When you assume this balanced position, you will have to depend upon the hands and arms solely to generate sufficient force against the sand to send the ball to the green. Above all, do not alter your body position during the use of the club or you will

154

do a number of things—all unpleasant.

This position will show you how beautifully and accurately your hands and arms can use the club; how well they can develop centrifugal force—speed—precisely at the point of contact with the ball. This is possible when a constant, flexible position is maintained with your body.

Fairway Trap

This shot demands that you strike the ball cleanly and sharply. It requires that you establish a *very sound body foundation* upon which to use the club. The speed which will be involved with a longer club—possibly a wood—will require such a foundation. Do not

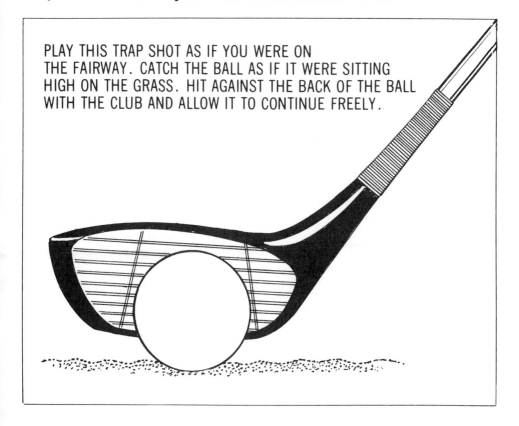

PLAY THIS TRAP SHOT AS IF YOU WERE ON THE FAIRWAY. CATCH THE BALL AS IF IT WERE SITTING HIGH ON THE GRASS. HIT AGAINST THE BACK OF THE BALL WITH THE CLUB AND ALLOW IT TO CONTINUE FREELY.

use your legs excessively or unnecessarily. Whenever your hips, legs and feet shift around, your foundation is destroyed.

Play this shot as if you were on the fairway. Catch the ball as if it were sitting high on the grass. Hit against the back of the ball with the club and allow it to continue freely. If you catch some sand during this effort, it should not be much, so don't worry. Your goal is to hit the ball at the target. The sudden force—impact, energy—should be at the ball to the finish as in other shots. Never use the club from the top with force or speed. Reserve this power for the bottom of the arc into the finish.

Goal: hit ball
at target

When you have mastered catching the ball cleanly without sand from the fairway traps, you will have learned how to hit the ball perfectly. If you desire to improve your game, this is a good place to start. Here all your shots must be hit perfectly and on balance. You will not be able to allow your body to squirm around and still hit the ball full out. Instead of practicing mechanical moves or theories, practice hitting the ball with long clubs from a fairway trap until you master the clean hit against the ball with sudden force.

On clearing
fairway trap

Many times you are faced with a long shot from the fairway trap but must also clear the mound or lip in front of the ball. Try a four iron with the blade open as your sand club. Face more to your left because the ball will fly to the right, or from left to right in a fade. Pick up the club more abruptly and use it against the ball cleanly in a cutting or lifting action. You will see the ball clear this obstacle, fly high and yet go the necessary distance. To execute this shot, your wrist must be very supple.

You have read earlier how to hold the club, assume balance, and place the club back in a calm manner for the purpose of striking the ball. This control is applicable in playing these shots. Be totally positive in every aspect. Remember when the ball is gone, you have no control over it. The only control you have is when you are at the ball. Therefore, control is all mental and never physical. When you have mastered these sand shots, you will discover that you have greater confidence in all other shots.

Consider all the trouble shots you have played well—under a tree, from a bad lie, in a deep depression, and over or around a tree. You choke the club short for some shots, balance with one leg up and one leg down for others, and from the side of hills punch the shot under branches. Why did you play such shots well and some easy ones badly?

Simply because you were concerned with the shot and controlled yourself mentally until the shot was hit. *You could not use the body in your favorite way, twist the shoulders, keep the left arm stiff, get off the feet and shift the weight—so you focused on the job at hand.* Thus you proved that the computer which God gave you really worked. *The body did adjust to the use of the club by the hands.* This is more than psychological nonsense. Trust these sound principles and play better golf.

Trouble shots
need skill

Tap It In

10

You have attacked the course from tee to green and somehow find yourself on the putting surface. You need a 20-footer for a par. This time everything works like a charm and "plop," the ball finds the hole.

"Why can't I do this every time?" you ask.

The answer may lie in one or more considerations. Do you always have an aggressive purpose, a balanced foundation for sinking the putt, a proper procedure for approaching the ball, an understanding of how to gather information necessary for making many putts within range, a method which eliminates apprehension and tension?

How to make putts within range

Is such a method available? Indeed it is.

The pressure to make a putt is as great as the pressure to hit good shots from tee to green. This is why there is a never-ending chase after the secret to successful putting. And a great many putting styles have developed.

One school of thought says, "Use your arms and shoulders as one unit with stiff wrists." Another in-

159

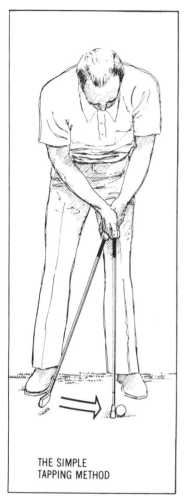

THE SIMPLE
TAPPING METHOD

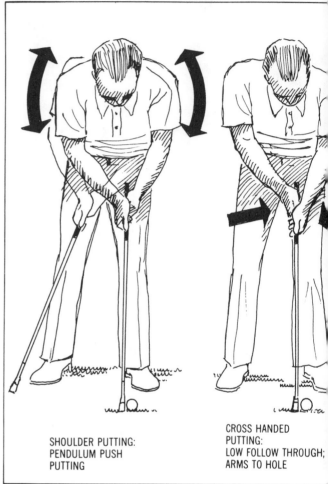

SHOULDER PUTTING:
PENDULUM PUSH
PUTTING

CROSS HANDED
PUTTING:
LOW FOLLOW THROUGH;
ARMS TO HOLE

sists, "Point your left elbow at the hole, keeping the left wrist in the bent position."

Other instructions pour out uninvited: "Hold the putter short and use the arm stiffly. Stroke the putt. Use the pendulum system. Push the putter through the ball. Keep the blade low along the ground back and forth. Bring the putter inside and move through with the

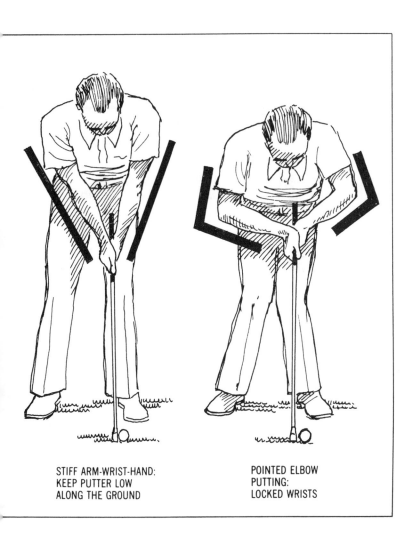

STIFF ARM-WRIST-HAND:
KEEP PUTTER LOW
ALONG THE GROUND

POINTED ELBOW
PUTTING:
LOCKED WRISTS

hands locked together. Place one hand way below the other on the club."

Regardless of the method you employ, you can improve your putting by learning to read the green. Does it slope left or right on the line of putt, away from the ball or toward the ball? Is the grain of the grass against you, away from you or across the line of putt?

As you approach the green, try to walk on a line with the ball and the flag. This not only will keep your mind occupied with the business at hand, but also will give you an overall impression of the green from the ball to the hole. You will have some idea of what you must do before you actually mark the ball, clean it and replace it in preparation for putting the ball to the hole. This helps you to concentrate on the reason for approaching the green: *to tap the ball into the hole.*

After cleaning and replacing the ball, look from

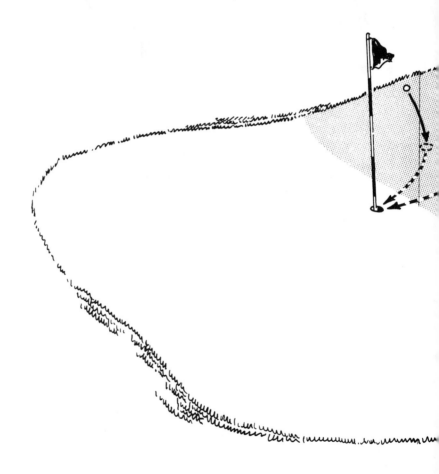

behind the ball for any slopes which will affect the motion of the ball to the hole, confirming the impression you gained as you approached the green. Walk to the lower side and check from that angle also. After doing so, determine at which point the ball will begin to be affected by the slope. Then you should putt the ball for this point as if it were actually the hole. This allows the slope to drift the ball to the hole. This is known as drift putting.

Never charge the ball on side slopes or on down

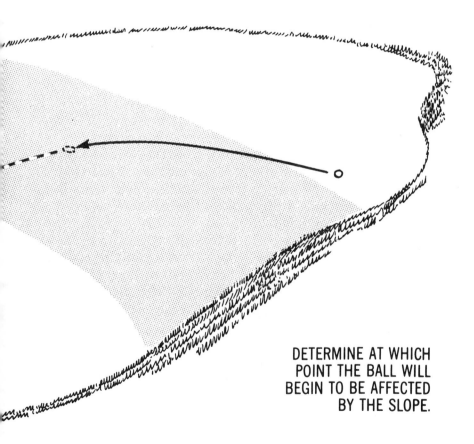

DETERMINE AT WHICH
POINT THE BALL WILL
BEGIN TO BE AFFECTED
BY THE SLOPE.

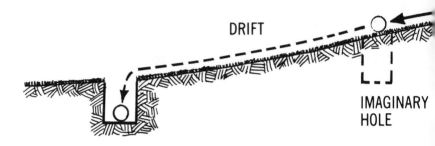

DRIFT

IMAGINARY
HOLE

slopes; you must remember that the ball will pick up speed as it descends the slope. If you have been three putting, this may be your problem. You should look into the cup to check the distance from the edge of the cup to the surface of the green. If one side is greater than the other, a slope will be present at the hole. This is important because the ball will be affected when it approaches the hole.

Allow putt to drift
    Allowing the putt to drift will cause you to borrow more from the slope than you normally would, and more times than not you will end up nearer the hole for an easy tap in. Moreover, you will discover that a drifting putt can often catch the side or the back of the cup and drop in.

When the slope is uphill from your ball, simply tap the ball to go beyond the hole. Do not think of hitting it harder. Just consider where the ball should end.

When the grain of the grass is against you (darker looking than when the grain is away from you), the ball will encounter resistance. When the grain is away from you the ball will roll with more speed.

164

PUTT

IF ONE SIDE
OF THE CUP
IS GREATER
IN DEPTH FROM
THE SURFACE
OF THE GROUND
A SLOPE WILL
BE PRESENT AT
THE HOLE.

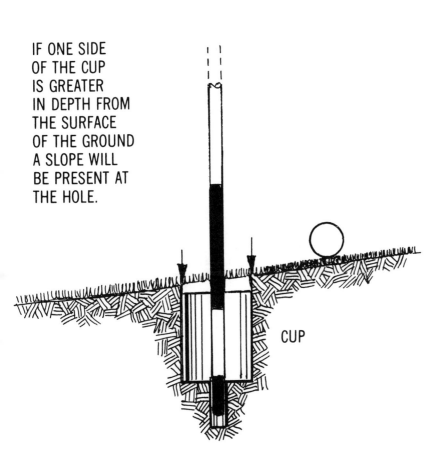

CUP

165

On a fast green, which is slick as a billiard table, with undulations in every direction, drift putting becomes very important. It requires the delicate procedure of tapping or bumping the ball to the hole. Tapping is superior to stroking. In stroking, the fear of sending the ball too far will cause a subconscious reaction to grab the putter.

Whether self-inflicted or from outside sources, pressure generates tension, fear and difficulty in focusing on the job at hand. A calm, aggressive attitude will allow you to respond to natural instincts. You will always be better off to admit the putt can be missed even though you desire to make it. In fact, any putt can be missed! Therefore ask yourself, "On which side of the hole do I desire to miss the putt?" This may sound negative, but in reality releases you from a hindering fear.

How to respond to natural instincts

This attitude has prevented many golfers from becoming negative about the end results. It allows them to respond to information gathered, moving the ball toward the side of the hole decided upon, then often watching the ball find the hole instead of lagging nearby. Your brain picked up information and demanded a response from your physical mechanism to send the ball to the hole. This is a natural response to thought. Your conscious effort to make the putt will many times be the reason for missing the putt. Concern over the end result can be extremely detrimental.

Excess concern detrimental

When you have impressed your God-given computer mind with information, trust it to stimulate the correct response to make the putt. Impress upon the "computer" your desire to miss the ball close to the hole if it cannot make the putt. As a result, watching the putt end close to the hole time after time will eliminate pressure and develop confidence in your ability. Then watch the ball roll into the hole time after time.

Now you will have developed a procedure by which

you organize yourself each time you approach the green. You will depend upon your eyes to dictate corrections as you do when driving your car and respond to them instinctively. You have created such a deep impression as to what you desire the ball to do, where it must travel, that you simply tap the ball on its way. Nothing else matters at that moment except tapping the ball. A calm, aggressive attitude will overcome tension that produces paralysis. Self-discipline results in freedom and control from putt to putt.

Self-discipline nets freedom

Fringe Putting

Many times you will be on the fringe of the green. This is known as frog hair—when the grass is short but not as short as on the putting surface. Here you can use a putter more successfully than an iron. This situation will prove the tapping method superior to all others.

Why? Usually the ball does not begin rolling immediately when tapped. It slides first, then begins to roll. Your tactic is to get the ball to the green so it can pick up natural overspin (we shall discuss this in more detail later in this chapter).

Suppose the ball ends up near the green but in a depression or hole. What club should you use to hit the ball to the green? Your putter often can be your best bet. Hood the blade of the putter so the face faces the ground. Place the ball off or behind the right foot. You will need to face the target more for this shot because the ball will go right. When ready, create a descending tap against the top back of the ball to pinch it against the ground and make it jump into the air. The ball will bounce out of the depression, clear the longer grass between the ball and the green, then roll very rapidly. The putter is better than an iron, which could leave the ball short of the green, scull the ball over the green, or hit the shot fat. Upon landing, the ball moves with con-

Using putter near green

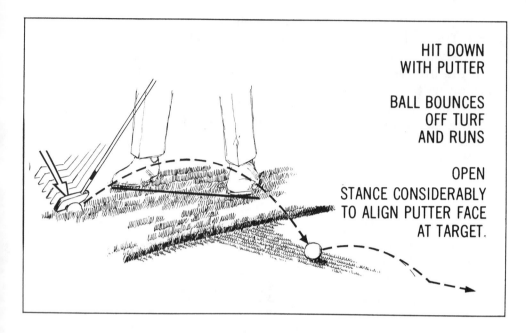

HIT DOWN
WITH PUTTER

BALL BOUNCES
OFF TURF
AND RUNS

OPEN
STANCE CONSIDERABLY
TO ALIGN PUTTER FACE
AT TARGET.

siderable speed. Learn how hard to tap the ball for a given distance and under all circumstances.

Balance

Now that you have accumulated the necessary information, you must assume a sound, balanced foundation upon which the putter can be used simply to tap the ball to the hole.

The balanced foundation   The easiest way for you to assume this foundation is to place the body weight on both feet, bend straight forward from the waist until the putter reaches the ground, keeping your head in the center of your stance. This means your eyes will be behind the ball so they can get a better view of the line from the ball to the hole. The head merely turns toward the hole; it does not lift or straighten up to allow the eyes to look at the line.

Place the right elbow so it touches the right front hip joint, allowing your forearm to cross the body to the left so the right palm is square to the hole near the left leg.

THE SIMPLE TAPPING METHOD

RIGHT ELBOW
AGAINST BODY.
RIGHT HAND
FLEXES AT
WRIST JOINT
FREELY.

THE LEFT ARM
IS THE
FLOATING ARM
TO RIGHT HAND
ACTION.

This will put the putter head even with the left heel. Place the left hand on the putter and allow the arm to hang flexibly at the side.

Now place the putter on the ground slightly back of the left heel. Both arms should be bent and flexible near the body.

This position allows the shoulders to be perfectly balanced without causing resistance to the action.

Use putter without tension When the arms are in this position, the hands and fingers can use the putter without tension. The knees bend. How much is determined by the length of the putter. Allow yourself to assume a calm, flexible position, one without tension, all muscles in an elastic, resilient attitude—a position of confident repose. After all, even touring professionals miss a putt now and then. Face this reality: you too will miss an occasional putt.

Women should normally use a 34-inch putter while men should use a 35- or 36-inch putter. There are variations in these lengths, of course, usually depending upon the height of the individual. I like a 36-inch putter because it allows the arms to bend at the elbows and keep close to the body, creating a firm center for the action.

When the wrists remain flexible, you have a center upon which to use the putter. The right hand is the con-

Right hand is controller trolling hand. The right arm does not move at the elbow when the putter is taken away from the ball. This will keep the putter from moving off line in either direction. When the arms are far from the body or they move a great deal, the hands do not have a center to work from, causing variations in the use of the putter.

The left arm and hand will float away from the body and follow the right hand and arm in their action. When the putter strikes the ball, the right hand will move forward and take the left hand and arm with it. Remember to keep your weight on both feet, body in a flexed position, left arm flexibly against the body and the right elbow anchored against the body, allowing the fingers to take the weight of the putter and tap the ball. This position will not require the body to move in order to compensate for a faulty action. You need only to remain in a sound balanced position.

Simple Tap

The fingers have tremendous sensitivity to what they touch. They sense the weight of the putter and will tell your mind whether the weight is too heavy, too light or just right.

Fingers sense weight

A golf instructor can fit you with a putter best suited to you. He will suggest the length best for you; the head style will probably be left up to you. I like the grip with a flat surface because it allows me to place the thumbs on top of the handle. The round portion under the grip is best for my feel, perhaps for yours also. This is known as the paddle type of grip. This will allow a more consistent feel in the fingers from day to day. You and you alone can decide which type is best for you.

Before you can tap the ball with the putter, you must understand how to hold the putter and what controls the action of the putter. If you were to putt with one hand—say, the right hand—you would hold the putter in the fingers with the thumb directly over the index finger. This relationship of the thumb and index finger creates a pinched feel which forms a figurative electrical circuit to the brain.

Putting with one hand

This is the way to learn how to putt: practice with the right hand only (or left, if you are left-handed), placing the right arm and hand in position by anchoring the right elbow as previously mentioned. Then tap the ball with the fingers using the blade. Notice the putter face remains absolutely square. Continue tapping the ball this way until this control and motion prove more accurate and simple than anything you have tried.

Although you may prefer the grip you now use, you should try the paddle grip to see if it improves your putting. I feel it is superior to other grips.

Place the club in your left hand, allowing the handle **Position** to rest against the side of the heel pad of your hand. In **of heel pad** your regular grip, the handle will be under this pad. When the fingers fold around the handle, the pressure points will be in the tips of the fingers. The left thumb rests on the top of the handle.

To place the right hand on the club, lift the left forefinger and slide your hand up the shaft until the forefinger folds over the third finger of the right hand. The little finger of the right hand folds over the second finger of the left hand. While the shaft rests in the

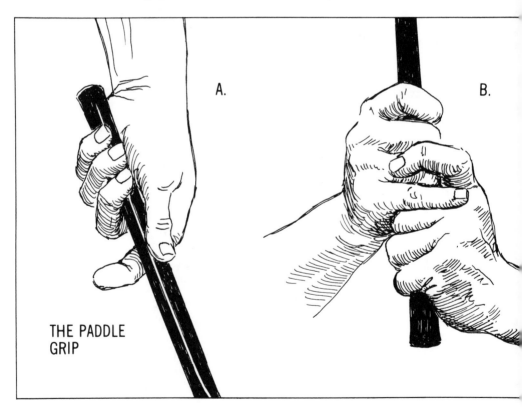

A.

B.

THE PADDLE
GRIP

cradle of your right forefinger, place your right thumb on top directly over the forefinger, pressing the heel pad of your right hand against the second finger of your left hand. The two hands are now balanced to the direction of the putter face. They will prevent the putter face from opening or closing. You will always have a putter face striking the ball squarely on the line chosen.

Balance hands on putter

The joint of the left thumb near the nail will sit under the thumb pad of the right hand. This position brings both hands close together, resulting in unified action. The position of your fingers gives you control and sensitivity to the putter. Your fingers are aligned on the handle to prevent them from squeezing the club unnecessarily. This assures a calm, resilient response.

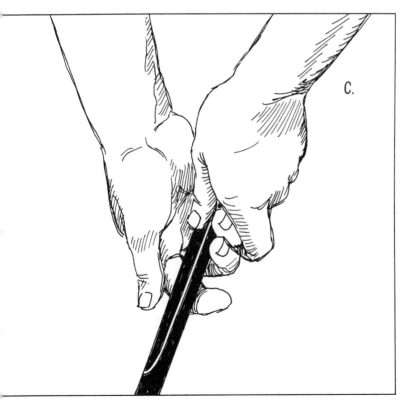

C.

Touch on the greens is impossible without sensitivity to the putter in your fingers. A clutching, stiff-wristed hold destroys control over the putter and tends to prevent one from playing calmly.

You can putt most greens more successfully when

Putting on sloping greens tapping the ball than when stroking the ball. You can strongly tap the ball uphill, against the grain, on slow greens, a long distance from the hole, or bump, nudge, or touch the ball on fast downhill sloping greens with equal accuracy. These adjustments in force against the ball do not require a change in action when using the tapping method. You will experience what is meant by "touch."

When you tap the ball, it will slide before picking up overspin. Because the face of the club remains square to the line of putt, no side spin will be imparted. The ball will not begin with overspin and run away from you out of control. In fact, when confronted with a very delicate downhill putt, you can drop the putter downward against the ball, causing it to hesitate momentarily and spin backwards before moving forward. This must be practiced before applying it on the course.

Wrists

What about wrist action? There is a myth regarding the use of wrists, particularly when putting. Some say they develop the "yips" because of being "wristy." The "yips" are a result of lack of confidence, or an overem-

Mechanical control overemphasis phasis on mechanical control. There is wrist motion in every golf shot you make, regardless of how slight it may be. Fluidity—the mark of a good golfer—cannot be achieved without wrist motion. The wrists bend only to accommodate the motion of the putter as directed by the fingers.

Point your finger to some object directly in front of you. Now point your finger, keeping it straight, to your right—then left. Did your wrist bend? Of course! Picture a club in your hand. You wish to point to your right then left. The response is the same. Try this again, keeping your arms stiff. It not only feels awkward but prevents any fluid motion of the clubhead. The same problem results when you attempt to use the putter with stiff wrists.

Understanding the Tap

You have a sound foundation and the correct placement of the fingers. What is left to do? Simply tap the ball.

Simply tap the ball

The quickest way to learn how to tap the ball is to ignore all the rolls at first, particularly on the practice green. In order to make use of the information you have gathered prior to balancing yourself over the ball, you must have a simple, sound method of tapping the ball. Tapping the ball to a given distance is most important. By ignoring all the rolls, you will learn the impact necessary for a given distance.

How do you tap forcefully without destroying calmness? How do you nudge the ball when on lightning fast greens? By learning that there is no force away from the ball or toward the ball—only at the point of contact. This will train you to focus on one thing only when the time comes to make the putt. Your eyes are flawless range finders. A calm attitude will keep the vision clear and enhance your instinct to tap the ball accurately. There is no need for speed or force, only a degree of aggressiveness against the ball.

Eyes flawless as range finders

You have decided to send the ball to the hole along a certain line. Why change your thought pattern now through conscious control of the mechanics, fear of the outcome, or other negatives? Your body does not stimulate the action. Your wrists do not stimulate the action. Your mind and fingers do. You cannot have two things on your mind when putting. Forget about the distance, roll, mechanical control, what is going on around you. You gather the information needed to make the play beforehand. When the time for action comes, simply concentrate on tapping the ball aggressively.

Right hand should dominate

Approach the ball in the same manner each time. Keep a positive attitude toward the hole. Allow the right hand to dominate the action. Continually tap the ball with the fingers. This kind of practice will develop control of the blade, squaring it automatically at impact. The centralized position will demand that the putter remain on line at all times. The mind and reaction of the fingers will square the putter face. Success is assured if the right elbow remains fixed on the way

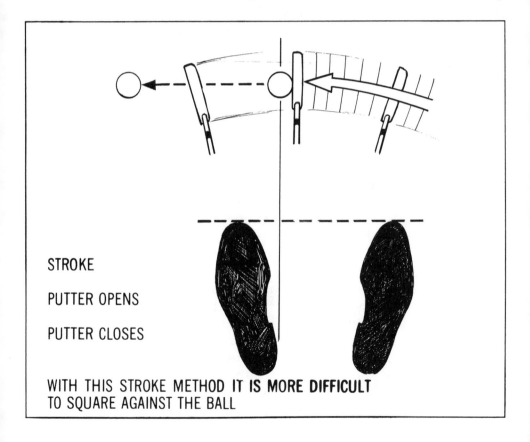

STROKE

PUTTER OPENS

PUTTER CLOSES

WITH THIS STROKE METHOD **IT IS MORE DIFFICULT** TO SQUARE AGAINST THE BALL back from the ball. This is the key to control.

Prove this to yourself! Tap the ball and hold the putter where it finishes. Notice that the blade is absolutely square. Were you to tap the ball, pull the blade back again immediately and hold the putter, you would notice that the blade is square. Tapping, striking, hitting or nudging the putter against the ball will keep the blade square. These actions do not imply muscular violence, strength or force, but activity of your putter head against the ball.

Keep the
blade square

When you stroke the ball, the putter can open or close if your motion is smooth and slow. The hands will have to roll over if you desire action.

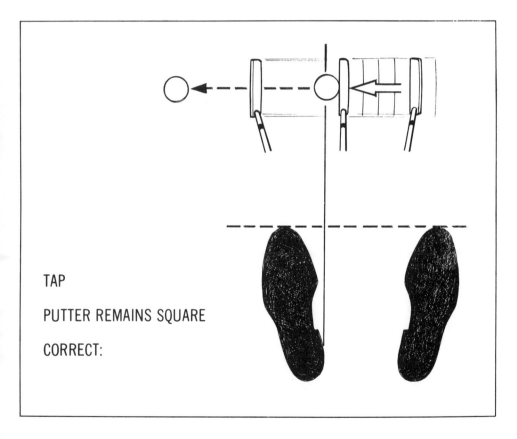

TAP

PUTTER REMAINS SQUARE

CORRECT:

Tap It In

You can now look forward to successful putting on all greens. You will not be haunted by embarrassment when you play a strange course. If you have difficulty sensing the putter weight, close your eyes after addressing the ball and tap the ball to where you last saw the hole. You will be amazed at how close you will come.

When teaching the blind, I line them up, tap the flag or hole and watch with astonishment as they putt to sound. Their accuracy is uncanny.

Another way to prove "how mental" putting is: address the ball, then look at the hole, and while looking at the hole tap the ball toward it. Again you will be surprised at your accuracy. In both instances you will notice the lack of concern over mechanical moves and control. You will notice how relaxed your muscles become, allowing you to coordinate for the purpose of tapping the ball.

You will enjoy many two-putt greens as a result of this simple method. Your disciplined attitude will pay immense dividends.

**THE AUTHOR
DEMONSTRATES
WEIGHT
BALANCE**

Something Is Missing

11

Are you blind or a victim of arthritis or cardiac? Do you have fingers missing, or a leg or an arm? Do you have bursitis or back problems? Have you had an operation which has destroyed or limited the use of one side or the other? Do you let a physical impairment keep you from playing golf?

The truth is that you can play a commendable game of golf with what you have available. In fact, handicapped persons often apply themselves far more than persons with all their faculties. The wonderful and infallible computer which God has given to all individuals (handicapped or normal) can coordinate perfectly for use of the golf club.

Handicap no deterrent

Right Arm

Let us suppose you have only a right arm. You will need to learn how to address the ball for your particular physical condition. However, the basics which we mentioned in an earlier chapter still apply to you. You must take into account that you have more strength in your one arm and hand than the person who has two arms. This is to your advantage.

Before thinking about position, check your clubs for weight and strength of shaft. You don't want a club which places a strain upon your arm and hand muscles. Test the weight to see if you can easily use it. You should have a shaft which allows the fingers to feel the weight in motion.

Check clubs for weight, strength

Now how do you position yourself at the ball for the greatest advantage? Each person must adjust the address position to his unique physical characteristics and allow instinctive coordination to the use of the club. There cannot be one specific position from which you can hit the ball.

To hold the club you must place it deep into the fingers of your hand with the large knuckle of the forefinger almost underneath the shaft. Place the thumb on top of the shaft with the handle underneath the pad of the back of the hand. This will provide a strong hold on the club with all of the fingers.

When the grip is secure, address the ball by bending from the waist first until the club reaches the ground. As suggested earlier, the knees should always bend last to support the weight of the upper portion of the body. The club should be positioned to allow the ball to be in line with or just behind the left heel. In many cases the ball can be slightly farther back than standard. The hand must have a slight angle at the wrist joint. The wrist must never be raised, or it will destroy the necessary coordination between the arm and hand. This is vital and must be adhered to at all times. The palm of the hand must face the target.

Knees should bend last

All fingers should have a firm hold upon the shaft. Now you are ready to place your feet into proper position for striking the ball. You might do better if the left foot is placed slightly in front of the right foot. Or

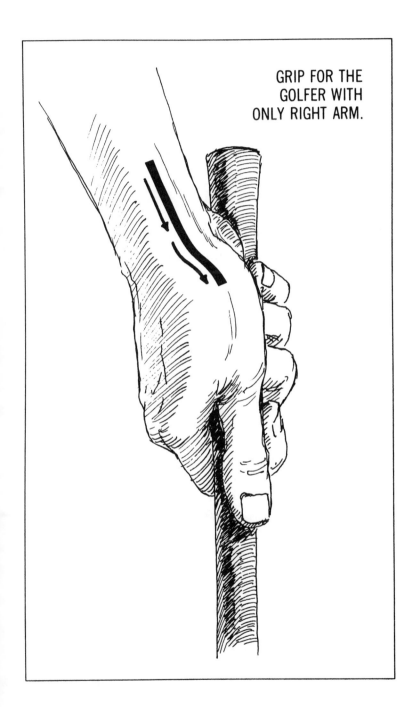

GRIP FOR THE
GOLFER WITH
ONLY RIGHT ARM.

after the feet have been placed on a parallel line to the flight of the ball, pull the right foot slightly back from that line. This will create what is known as a closed stance. You should not exaggerate this position. This foundation will allow you to use the right hand and arm with greater force against the ball. Your weight should be more to the left. The head and shoulders remain over the ball.

Keep weight to the left

You should never allow your weight to shift to the right when taking the club away from the ball. The right leg braces the body and should continue to brace when the club is at the top. This body position and balance will help you to move the club against the ball for more accuracy and distance.

From this firm, sound foundation, you must use the club with singleness of purpose and control. Whatever you do, never allow your feet to lose full contact with the ground. Whenever you make a move which causes you to balance on a small portion of your feet, such as the toes or heels, you will not be able to generate force against the ball at impact.

Keep feet on the ground

Do not take the club back with tension, strength, force or speed. The body should be ready, flexible and resilient to coordinate with the club at impact and move with it into the finish. When you allow the body to adjust itself to the club in a shoulder-high position slightly behind you, you will discover that the body has turned immediately in the same position over the ball. The left knee has bent slightly and the weight is on both feet so you can strike with force at the bottom of the swing.

Force at bottom of swing

Try an experiment. Clench your fist, placing the fist above your right shoulder and bending the wrist backward. Your right arm will be almost horizontal to the ground. Keep the wrist coiled as you bring the hand and arm downward in front of your body waist high. At this point snap your wrist flexibly and suddenly, allow-

184

DO NOT TAKE
THE CLUB BACK
WITH TENSION,
STRENGTH, FORCE
OR SPEED.

EXPERIMENT
DESCRIBED
ON PAGE 184

ing your arm to bend as well. Place all effort at this point. The sudden snap must be timed for the bottom of the swing only. Do not allow your fingers to open up.

As you place the fist in the top position independently, so should you place the club independently. As you move the hand and arm downward, do likewise when the club is in your hand. Then, the arm is bent at the top to help generate more club head force circularly.

Do not use body in placing club If you use the body to help place the club at the top, shift weight, and make deliberate shoulder turns, you will be out of position and must attempt to return to that position in which you originally addressed the ball. These moves away from the ball demand moves toward the ball which are detrimental to timing. Therefore, you must always place the club in a balanced, coiled, poised position for striking the ball with the right hand and arm, allowing the body to respond to their movement.

When you are ready to attack the ball, you should begin your descent with the same calm attitude you assumed when placing the club back. This will tend to keep your body in a flexible condition so that at the point of impact it will move with the club in a synchronized action.

Body should not lead hand, arm Never allow the body to lead the hand and arm toward the ball. The body automatically moves left to balance the effort of the hand and arm against the ball. This is a reflex action. The club moves without strength when the body leads. For example, place the club in a poised position. Hold the hand and arm in this position and lead with the body. Note several reactions. The hand and arm cannot generate force against the ball. The body is off balance and this disturbs the timing.

When the body leads, the shoulders move on a different line than the intended line of flight. The body pulls the right arm, dragging the club after it. The hand cannot use the club for striking the ball, so it holds tight

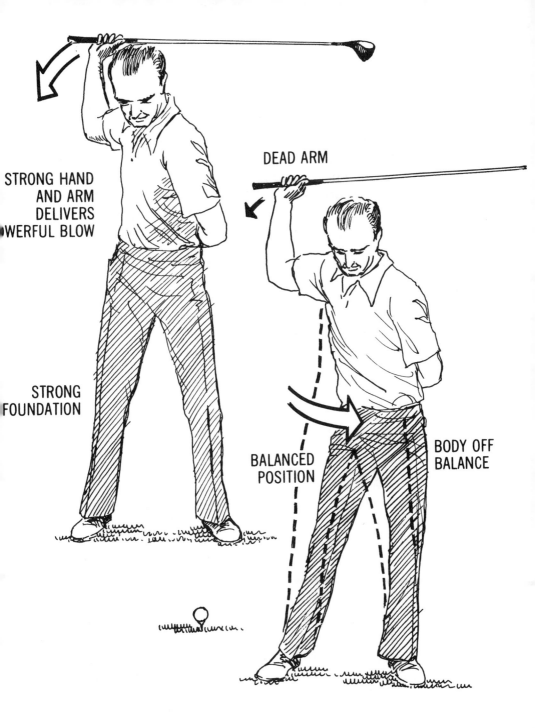

STRONG HAND
AND ARM
DELIVERS
WERFUL BLOW

STRONG
FOUNDATION

DEAD ARM

BALANCED
POSITION

BODY OFF
BALANCE

187

and pulls the shaft, dragging the club head at and through the ball in a very weak, fluffy hit.

Once again place the club in a poised position. This time keep the body firmly balanced on both feet, allowing the hand and arm to proceed toward the ball in a calm manner for striking the ball at the bottom of the arc. This balanced foundation allows the weight of the body to be used in conjunction with the club head, adding force against the ball. Notice the contrast between the two actions—one a weak confused movement, the other a well-balanced, forceful action against the ball.

Use cardboard box in practice

Practicing against an empty cardboard box will develop proper synchronization from the ball, back to the ball. It will help to develop the habit of hitting against the side of the ball. It will also teach you how to determine when the force is needed and at which point it should be applied. Most important of all, the practice will alert you to the fact that you give little conscious thought to moves made away from the box, back to the box, and how you have focused your attention on the contact with the box. You did not have your attention focused upon mechanical moves.

Never keep the arm stiff

When the club strikes the ball, the hand and arm should follow the club, giving with the motion. Never keep the arm stiff so the club cannot move with freedom through the ball. Such a movement of the arm will create resistance to the motion of the clubhead.

All clubs, including those for the short game, are controlled in the same manner. The shorter the club, the more you will need to bend from the waist. Shorter irons demand a different position of the feet. You do not need distance and, therefore, a long backward move is not necessary. When the body bends more from the waist, the backward move is curtailed. Never try to place the club back farther than the body will allow when in this position.

The ball should be placed more in the center of the

stance for an individual with a right arm only. The ball would be off the left foot for an individual with the left arm only. The feet should be more square to the line of flight than with the longer irons. Your body weight now feels as though it were on the left side. The left hip is shoved slightly to the left. You take the club and sharply hit the ball at the precise position where the ball rests on the ground.

Shove left hip to the left

The closer you get to the green, the shorter you hold the club and the more you use your hand. Focus still on the point of impact, hit sharply at the ball, with the arm closer to your body than when hitting a longer shot.

Also, the closer you get to the green, the closer together you bring your feet. Your weight should still rest on your left side. Regardless of the distance, your purpose is to hit the ball to a given target at all times. This shot requires more of an independent action of the hand, using the forearm around the upper arm, than the full movement of the entire arm.

Independent action of hand

Chipping from the edge of the green demands the use of the hand and forearm almost exclusively. Your upper arm rests against the side or slightly in front of your body, acting as a fulcrum. The club strikes the ball sharply for backspin so it will hold the line for accuracy.

For use of the sand wedge, review the chapter "Pressure the Ball Out." Your hand firmly in command, lift the head of the sand club abruptly and bang it into the sand, creating sufficient force to push the sand between the ball and club, lifting the ball onto the green. The distance the ball must travel determines the amount of force applied against the sand.

Bang club head into sand

The follow-through for all these shots is a result of the amount of impact needed against the sand to send the ball a given distance. Do not produce a mechanical, false follow-through. Focusing upon striking the sand with the club does not mean you stop the action of your hand and arm upon contact with the sand.

Putting is the same as described in the chapter on that subject. You should be a better putter than those with two hands. The ball is tapped with the head of the putter. When on the fringe of the green, the putter is often the best club to use.

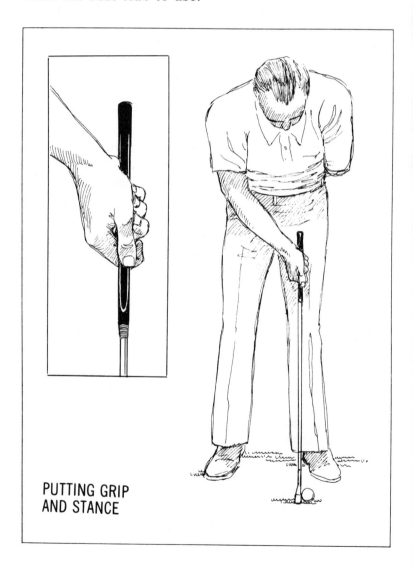

PUTTING GRIP
AND STANCE

Use the same balance described in the chapter on putting. Anchor the right elbow in front of and against the body just in front of the hip. Allow the forearm to angle to the left and place the putter on the ground with the hand. The palm is square to the line of flight. When the arm is anchored, the hand can use this as a center of operation.

You do not have another hand and arm to contend with and, therefore, should putt better than your two-armed colleagues. The use of the putter does not require movement of the entire arm back and forth. Too much movement is dangerous. Simply use a sharp tap.

One arm can be better

Actually, when following the method described in this book, you will be organized from shot to shot. You should always assume an aggressive, positive attitude at all times. Above all, you must respond to the God-given computer which is without equal—your mind.

Left Arm Only

For an individual with only a left arm, the purpose for using the club remains the same as for the individual with the right arm only. The action may vary somewhat, but never the purpose.

The club is placed into the fingers, placing the handle under the fatty pad of the heel of the hand. The large knuckle of the forefinger sits over on the left side of the handle while the thumb sits on the right of the handle. This provides a stronger hold upon the club. This is not a good grip for those with two arms and hands. The angle of the hand to the arm is retained at all times. The wrist is never raised.

How to get stronger hold

The alignment of the feet is similar to that of the individual with only a right arm. The ball is placed off the left heel. The balance of your body weight is the same as for the individual with only the right arm.

The left hand and arm place the club in a poised position shoulder high, in line with the body or slightly

191

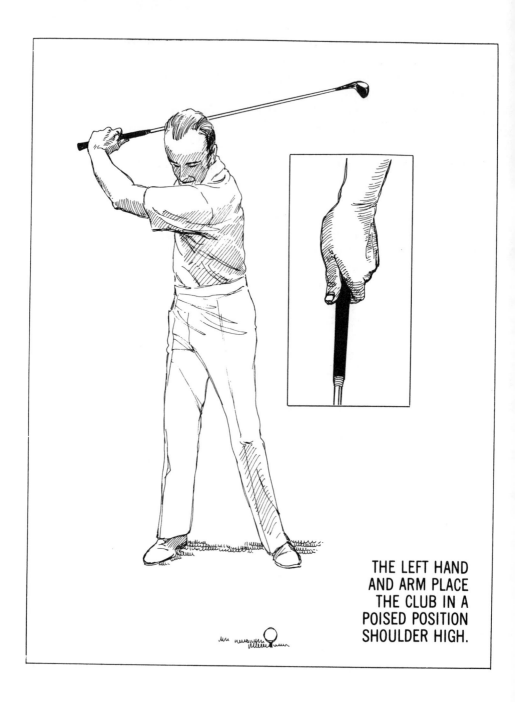

THE LEFT HAND
AND ARM PLACE
THE CLUB IN A
POISED POSITION
SHOULDER HIGH.

between the right shoulder and head. Never place the club above the shoulders. The body remains in its position over the ball as the club is placed in the preparatory position for striking the ball. When placing the club, the hand pulls the arm which pulls the shoulder until it is in front of the chin. Your shoulder movement should not be deliberate, rather an instinctive response. The left knee bends automatically, never deliberately. When this is a responsive action, the body will be soundly balanced and ready to assist the force of the club.

In placing the club back observe the same instructions as for the individual with only a right arm. Always perform all movements away from the ball and toward the ball in a calm manner. This will help you pinpoint attention on the ball while retaining an aggressive attitude for the use of the club. Remember, the arm moves independently from the body and is the motivating force for all body movements. It is not the body moving the arm, but the arm moving the body.

Try this experiment. Assume your stance, make a fist, have the arm extend down and out in front of you. Imagine that something solid is even with your left leg or place a real pillow there. Place the back of the hand against this imaginary object or pillow. Calmly take the back of the hand away from the pillow and crunch it by smashing the hand against it. *Be sure to make believe or use something soft as the pillow.* The force should be against the object only.

This exercise will help you time the force and body coordination. You produce this action instinctively and with little or no thought over mechanical movements involved. It is performed in a flexible, coordinated, yet powerful motion. The reaction should be the same when holding a golf club in your hands. Never use a strong or stiff left arm. Allow it to extend straight from the pull and action of the club, but do not lock it stiffly.

Shoulder moves instinctively

Use pillow for experiment

193

With a club in your hand, apply this action and thought against an empty cardboard box, one which gives easily against the force of the club head. Use an old club for this purpose. You may concentrate on the words *right* and *there* as you hit the ball, for greater timing of the force. The word *right* is prolonged; the word *there* is sharp and forceful at the point of impact.

A sharp hit develops backspin and determines the amount of follow-through. When the club has struck the ball, you must allow the arm to follow the head of the club into the finish. Some individuals keep the arm strong all the way into the finish. It is better if you allow the arm to remain firm naturally as the force is developed and bend more in the finish. The arm turns the body into a full finish.

Keep arm naturally firm all the way

The more you allow the arm to cooperate with the weight of the club in motion, the faster the weight moves and the farther the ball travels. A strong or stiff arm will resist the action of the club and create tension in other parts of the body as well. Wrist-bending is at a minimum when using long clubs due to the force involved. The wrist becomes more active as the shots get closer to the green.

Some individuals with only the left arm have large pectoral muscles which force the arm away from the chest. When this is the case, you might have to turn more on the way back or place the club in a position no farther back than you can comfortably coordinate with and retain balance. If the shoulder is pulled too far right, an exaggerated move to the left may occur, moving you past the position you originally had over the ball and resulting in one of a dozen errors. This individual will be better organized by placing the club in a lower position on the backward movement. He will better coordinate his body to the forceful use of the club head against the ball.

Watch extent of shoulder move

The closer you get to the green, the more you can experiment with the placing of the arm and hand for chip shots. Many golfers place the hand and arm even with the left leg, or to the left of the leg, or just inside the leg, according to individual preference. The combined use of the arm and hand diminishes as the ball is closer to the green. A chip shot does not demand a large action; therefore, the hand will control the club. Sharply pop the ball to the green. Use the same procedure as mentioned in the chapter on "Stroke Savers." The sand play is the same as mentioned in the chapter, "Pressure the Ball Out."

Putting is easy when performed simply. Some place the ball even with the left toe, some to the left of the toe, and some in line with the left heel. Some hold the putter very short and keep the arm rather straight, while others hold the putter full length and bend the arm, using the hand more than the arm. You must experiment for yourself. I recommend that you place the ball off the toe or slightly left of the toe. This will provide better vision of the line to the cup.

Hit ball sharply to the green

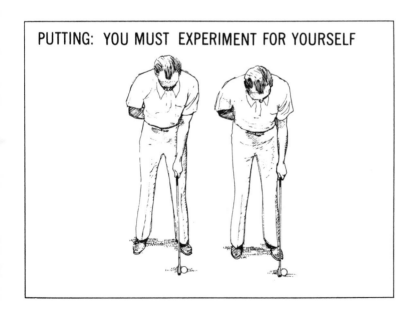

PUTTING: YOU MUST EXPERIMENT FOR YOURSELF

Your feet are square to the line and your weight on both feet. You must tap, pop, or bump the ball to the hole. Do not *stroke* the putter against the ball. No pendulum action of arm and hand is needed. Instinctive action results from an aggressive attitude of tapping the ball to the hole. If God created a machine which operates automatically in many areas of your life, He certainly has made it possible for the same control to work on your behalf in golf.

God's control can work for you

Only One Leg

Golfers with one leg must apply the free use of the hands and arms. The position of your hands upon the club is covered in previous chapters. The position of the ball will be opposite the toe regardless of whether it is your left or right toe. Some individuals prefer turning the toe slightly toward the target for better balance to the use of the club against the ball and into the finish. You must decide which position offers better balance.

Decide position for balance

The club is placed on the ground by bending from the waist, allowing knee bend to adjust instinctively. Your body must stop bending as soon as the club touches the ground. *This is of utmost importance, because it determines the elevation from which you use the club.* When you diminish the elevation or distance of the shoulders to the ground, the freedom of hand and arm action is hindered. The body will have to readjust to allow this freedom through the ball, destroying accuracy and force against the ball.

When properly balanced over the ball, you should focus attention against the back of the ball for a forceful smash of the club head. To accomplish this force, you must calmly place the club—shoulder high from the ball—with your hands. When you have placed the club at the top, allow the hands and arms to descend calmly toward the ball, generating force as they near the bottom of the arc. By retaining a resilient attitude

Focus for forceful smash

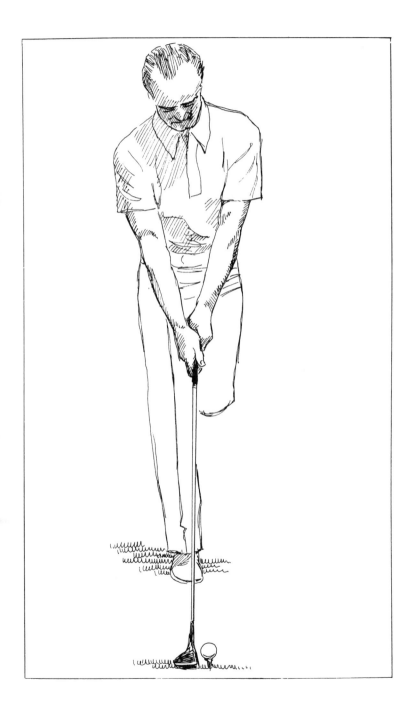

with your hands and arms, you can crunch the weight of the club against the ball and continue unhindered to the finish. The hands must be able to easily bend at the wrist joints for a snapping, lightning attack against the ball. You must use your hands a great deal, totally independent of body help as if you use nothing else.

Allow body to coordinate

Your body must be allowed to coordinate to the use of the club by the hands and arms. The amount of finish (for all shots) is determined by the amount of impact required to send the ball a given distance. When force is applied in this manner, you will notice the speed of the club diminishes as it continues past the ball. The

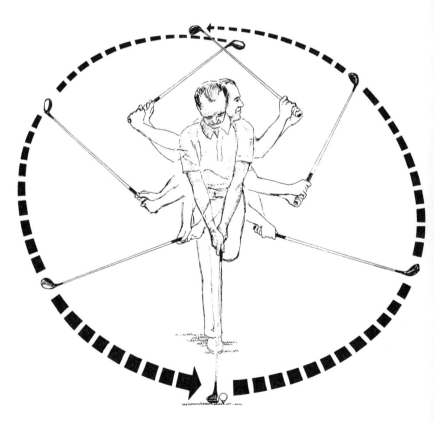

amount of backward motion is determined by the amount of impact necessary.

All shots will be hit sharply, the arms coordinating with the hands. However, *the club head must be used more with your hands than with the arms in either direction.*

The closer you get to the green, the shorter you hold the club and the more you use your hands. This sequence of action—hands, arms, then body—will allow your body to remain a well-balanced center ready to coordinate to the use of the club head for centrifugal force and power against the ball, resulting in a well-balanced finish.

Adjust when closer to green

Having only one leg will not deter you from playing all shots mentioned in earlier chapters. Apply the instructions as stated regardless of your situation. The use of your hands, arms, and body will not be hindered just because you have only one leg. You can perform on one leg as well and as efficiently as those on two legs. Use much wrist action while keeping the fingers on the club at all times. This will create more club movement, more arc, more impact. Your attitude to attack the course must never diminish. Stay *aggressive, alive!*

Only one leg need not hinder

Aggressiveness does not require that you handle the club with a strong grip or stiff muscles. This approach will cost you balance and speed. Your timing will not be accurate. All your aggressiveness must be with the head of the club against the ball toward the target, never away from the ball or down toward the ball. When you apply speed, strength, or stiffness in the swing away from the ball, your body cannot maintain balance or coordinate to the use of the club head. You will alter your position or perform resisting movements against the action of the club.

Be aggressive against ball

Take the natural way to better golf—the calm, flexible, synchronized use of muscles for force and accuracy. Your game will improve immensely.

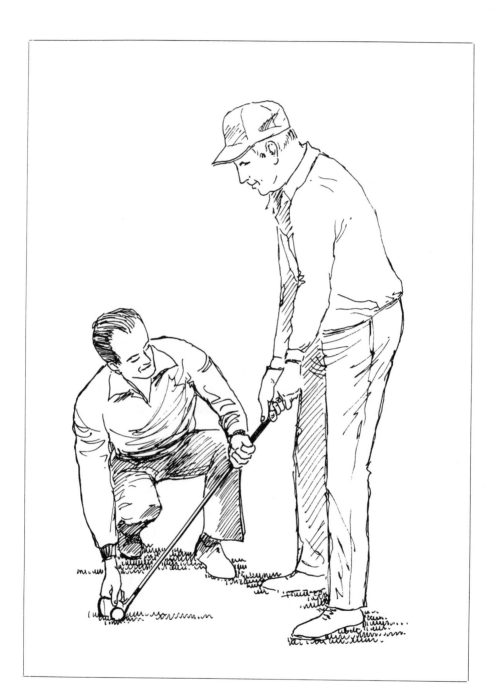

Yes, the Blind
Can Play Golf

12

An individual who has lost his sight is apt to feel that he cannot play golf. This is far from the truth! It hurts me to think of the many who are depriving themselves of the pleasures of golf because they don't know this.

My teaching experience with men and women who have lost their sight is among the most rewarding in my career. Playing with them and teaching them is a pleasure for which I thank God.

Just as you may need to have someone read this book to you, so you will need to have someone with you to line up the club to the hole, tell you the distance you must traverse, select the club for the distance and eventually tell you where the shot landed.

Hold the club in the manner described in the chapter on balance. Use the same understanding of arm and hand relationship, bending the body from the waist first to place the club upon the ground and allowing the knees to bend accordingly.

Learning to identify the placement of the ball is the

Have someone tell distance

next step. Take the club in your hands as your aide holds the club in line for the shot. Then walk up to the club until your body rests against the handle. If the hands touch the center of the body, you have the ball placed too far toward the center. The hands, especially the left hand, should press against the inside of the left leg near the abdomen. This will put the ball off the left heel. (Your helper can probably tell you whether the placement is correct or not. However, you should try to become as independent as possible. This will help you play better golf.)

Become
independent

When this hand position has been established, make certain you feel that you are facing the club squarely. Then back away until there is sufficient freedom to allow your arms to move without coming against the body during the golf swing. You will bend at the waist as you step back.

When you back away, the shaft should remain where originally placed. Also, the handle should not be lifted or moved to the right or left of the original position. Remember to place the club toe slightly off the ground. Bend your knees only the amount necessary for balancing the upper portion of the body depending on the length of the club. This applies for all clubs, as mentioned in the chapter on body balance and grip. Recall your hand positions—extended toward the left leg.

The club is resting on the ground before you, the hands below your head and shoulders. Calmly proceed to place the club shoulder high—as high as is comfortable. Practice without a ball in order to reach the best position possible without disturbing your balance when placing the club back.

Hands below
head, shoulders

Should your hands and arms be placed lower than shoulder high? Should they move around in back of you, or more in front of you? The trial and error method is the best judge. Your assistant should indicate where coordination is best for you. However, you will be able

202

to tell. Do your hands and arms feel correct in distance from the body when you bring them back toward their original position at address?

You should sense when the hands and arms reach about the same level as their starting point. It is at this point that you focus your attention on hands and club action where the ball is resting on a tee or on the ground. This understanding will aid your ability to time the hit more accurately.

Learn to focus your attention upon the area from which the hands and arms originally began. It is in this area that you mentally stimulate the use of the club. After you have placed the club at the top position, begin the swing down toward the ball and apply all force when the weight reaches the point of impact. Your body should remain prepared to move from this point with the club into the finish along with the hands and arms. *Where to focus your attention*

Your body should end up where it originally began when moving the club away from the ball. Any excessive movement will make it difficult for you to remain balanced or use the club face with accuracy.

When the body is allowed to remain in a centralized position away from the ball, the left arm will pull the left shoulder into position and bend the left knee automatically. You will feel balanced and prepared for the club to descend toward the ball so you can help the hands and arms to the finish. *There should be independent action of the hands, arms and club, moving to the top away from the ball. The body remains ready for its return and assists at impact to the finish.* This is the correct feel and thought. *Move to top away from ball*

Practice this move from the position at address, and wait for the return to this area before going into action. The body must be a centralized, responding mechanism rather than a swaying, shifting or resisting mechanism.

Distance can be mastered only through practice with

one who can help judge it for you. *Control must be in your hands.* You can practice shorter irons (which do not demand a full action) by having someone tap the flag pole so you can relate the sound to distance. This is not used for a full shot, but for a pitch, pitch-and-run,

Practice to the sound

and simple chip shots. You will probably be holding your club shorter and can practice to the sound, having your friend tell you how far short or long you are.

Do not become concerned over accuracy at this point. Simply attempt to hit the ball for the right distance. Focus on the amount of impact that is required to send the ball to the sound. This will automatically determine

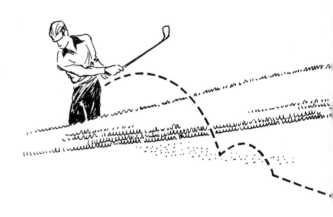

FOCUS ON THE AMOUNT OF
IMPACT REQUIRED TO SEND
THE BALL TO THE SOUND.

the amount of backward motion necessary. Each time you hit the ball, have your friend pace the yardage the ball traveled so you then can relate the impact with the distance. Practice hitting to faint sound, medium loud and loud sound. This will help you develop a true sense of distance.

Hitting to the sound will also apply when the ball is on the fringe of the green and on the putting surface. You should always putt to the sound, chip to the sound, and pitch-and-run to the sound.

Putt, chip, pitch-and-run

Use the putter as described in the chapter on putting. You will be able to eliminate many hindrances if you adhere to those instructions. This simple method eliminates all unnecessary actions that disturb your instinctive ability to react and respond to the situation. Your assistant describes the line and distance of the roll and then places your putter so it will allow for the drift to the hole. This is also explained in the chapter on putting.

The sand work of a blind person is marvelous to watch. You can learn to use the sand club (as described in the chapter on sand work) according to various lies which you will confront in the sand. However, you must have your friend hold the club so you can identify the position and place the ball correctly opposite the left heel.

Work your feet into sand

Work your feet into the sand so you can sense its texture. Is the sand wet, coarse, hard under the surface or soft? This foot maneuver will allow you to sense how the club must meet the sand to push the ball out. Again, your friend must tap the flag for sound and then tell you how far or short you are with your shot. With the hump of the wedge, practice putting different amounts of force against the sand, until you know the amount necessary to send the ball the distance of the sound.

If you are off the line, he can tell you how much correction you must make in your stance. Usually it will be to face more to the left. Practice the different shots mentioned in the sand chapter until you have confidence in playing them.

Ignore mistakes to overcome fear

Learn to accept mistakes and continue to practice regardless of how many mistakes you make. This is the only way you will overcome fear. Never consider mechanical moves as the cause for your error. You simply did not hit the ball right. Take the club with your hands and attempt to be more precise in timing its use against the ball.

You must acquire a personal sense of the action which suits you best. The only way this can be accomplished is through disciplined thought which will allow you instinctively to apply control over the club through your hands and arms, smashing the weight of the club *at one point for a specific purpose: to hit the ball where it rests.* All force and effort is to be applied in this area. You and you alone can coordinate your body. No two people perform physically and think mentally exactly alike. Honor God for this fact and you will play better golf.

You alone can coordinate your body

Dave Meador, a blind golfer, could be a champion some day. He applies these principles to perfection.

"There is no question, Gus," he said to me one day, "your approach to the game, your emphasis on the extreme importance of the hands and the golf swing, the importance of 'feel' throughout the swing, the importance of keeping the body passive until impact, and your clarity of explanation—all of these have changed my concept toward every shot. Your lessons will continue to improve my game for many tournaments to come."

Because most blind people have developed keener hearing they must learn how to cope with disturbing sounds. Develop complete absorption in the job at hand. Practice identifying which direction sound comes from and its distance from you. When ready to strike the ball, however, all noises should be blocked out.

Coping with disturbing sounds

On the course, assume an aggressive, attacking attitude which cannot be disturbed by incidentals. You have overcome and mastered many circumstances in your life. Golf is no different. You know where the ball is; just go about your business to hit it with the club head. Hit the ball in one direction only (toward the target, not away from the ball) and hit it with force at the bottom of the arc where the ball rests.

Have a good game.

Assorted
Physical Problems

13

Heart or Respiratory Ailments
If you have a heart condition or suffer from bronchial trouble, you must use the club with as easy a motion as possible. That's why the method I have been describing has met with such success—especially with persons having physical disabilities.

One man I had coached, E.C. Stork, wrote me: "I thought you would be interested to know that in May I had open-heart surgery involving two arterial by-passes. Seven weeks after leaving the hospital I was back playing golf. I do not feel I would have been able to return to the game as rapidly if it had not been for the swing you developed for me.

The swing is the thing

"Your approach as a teaching professional is different from anything we have previously experienced—resulting in great improvement for both my wife and me. This improvement gives us much added pleasure and enjoyment of the game."

If you have a breathing or heart problem, you cannot afford strain upon your heart. You must allow your hands and arms to move from the shoulder joints freely and without tension at any time during the action.

You must never allow tension when reaching the backward position. You should never increase effort and muscle strength toward the ball, but sense the weight of the club and move in unison with it, particularly when it strikes the ball to the finish. Your

Move in unison with club

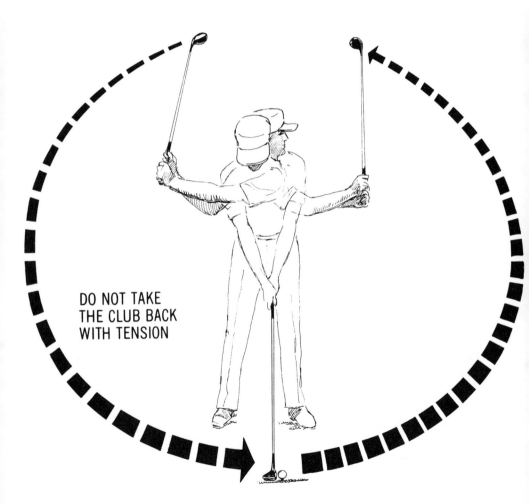

DO NOT TAKE
THE CLUB BACK
WITH TENSION

body action rhythmically conforms to the action of your hands and club.

You must feel your body as a flexible center upon which the hands and arms will use the club to strike the ball. Allow the body to adjust itself to this motion and feel a part of it from the ball into the finish.

Extensive backward motion must not be attempted. A free motion of the arms must be accomplished in either direction—particularly backwards. This motion on the way back sets the stage for the synchronized return toward the ball, against the ball, and your move into the finish. It is developed by the weight of the club.

Weight of club affects swing

Avoid too much leverage action of the wrists which tends to tense the forearms and causes you to tighten the grip while the club is moving. Your hands must remain free and active at the wrists. You must remain resilient when the club is back and be ready to respond toward the ball in the same attitude. This coordinated effort will increase the speed of the club without conscious muscle strain and will not demand added work on the part of the heart.

Stand at ease. Hold the club as if it were a friend. Use it with respect and care. Play the sport rather than attempting to overcome an enemy. Enjoy the flight of the ball regardless of distance gained. As you continue to adjust to this kind of thinking and club control, you will increase distance.

Finish with free balance, void of tension. Never overdo it on any day. Play only a few holes at a time and stay off the course in hot and humid weather. Proper hold on the club, ball placement, body balance and related matters have been covered earlier.

Advanced Years

When you are at a period in life when you no longer can manipulate your body as freely as you previously could, you must reevaluate your thought patterns—and

Reevaluate thought patterns

perhaps you should reevaluate your equipment too.

Take the equipment first. Does it allow you to use the clubs easily without strain or muscle tension? I would suggest you look for a club which has a shallow head and long face. A shallow head will help you get the ball into the air more easily. Ask for a 12- or 13-degree loft in the driver.

Correct length, strength and weight

Also ask for increased loft in your fairway woods. Consider the possibility of numbers six, seven and eight woods to replace irons you formerly used. Make sure the length of the club, strength of the shaft, and weight are correct for you. A golf professional is qualified to help fit you properly. You will be able to control the longer club more easily and hit the ball better and develop more confidence for these shots.

Second, you probably do not have the same strength you once had, but you can still coordinate whatever is available to you to play a fine game of golf.

Many golfers have asked me how they can break habits formed in an effort to perform what they considered correct movements—movements which they were never able to master. Begin by realizing that anything you do in life is accomplished through thought patterns. Thus when you change your thinking, you also change your physical reactions. Golf is no exception. The physical response to this thought change may feel awkward at first, but you will soon adjust to it.

Change your thinking

When you change the use of the club against the ball, your body must adjust its reaction as well. Repetition of proper thought is the key to success—shot after shot, hole after hole, day after day—not strength, ability, youth or athletic prowess.

Through intelligent thought, you can use the right club to send the ball close to the flag and make the putt. By maintaining flexible, resilient movement of the body, coordinated to the action of the hands and arms,

Flexible, resilient movement helps

you can still hit the ball fairly long and play shots which allow you to score well.

Mechanical golf moves you made for many years, and which you practiced diligently, now suddenly are hindering you simply because you cannot perform them. If you can't use them at this juncture in life, they certainly were not correct at the time you developed them. So keep an open mind and break these bad habits.

For instance, one man complained of physical fatigue and mental frustration after 18 holes of golf. When I observed him, I could see that he bent his knees deeply and used strong body turns to get the club back and through the ball. In addition, he attempted to develop speed and power by throwing the weight of the body ahead of the club. He made such a turn on the way back that he was on his toes and was pulled off the position he assumed over the ball at address.

He had difficulty keeping his attention on the ball because he moved so much. When he had gotten around, he would attempt to pivot left, hold on with the left hand, create a strong left arm, keep the right close to the body, and then make a full turn into the finish, holding the club stiff at the wrists. No wonder he was completely exhausted at the end of a round.

With some instruction he learned how to hold the club so that motion returned to the wrist joints. Now he could feel the weight of the club. He learned to allow the arms to move as freely as they could from the shoulder joint and as far back as they could. From this position he learned to allow the arms to reverse their action while his body waited to assist them at the point of impact and move with them into the finish. The arms moved without tension and without strength from the ball to the top and back to the ball. Then they could proceed with the speed they picked up naturally as they approached the ball into a balanced finish. This man

Hold club right; motion returns

greatly improved his game and at an advanced age still enjoys playing.

One afternoon I was giving a lesson when several individuals well up in years came to the practice range for help. One of them told about a secret maneuver he had once learned but had since forgotten. He wanted to learn how to get it back. The secret was this: when the left arm increased its strength and tension at the ball, he could hit farther and more accurately. Regrettably, he was now hitting the ground so hard that his arms and shoulders were in pain.

Another man claimed that his secret had been to place his left hand over the handle more and to roll the hand over at impact, following through with a strong rolling of the left arm into the finish. Regrettably, he was now shanking the ball and couldn't understand why.

The third fellow's former expertise had been in using a strong left arm to lift the left shoulder. He had also been told to stand unnaturally far from the ball.

The first golfer had to learn that any stiffness will resist motion and centrifugal force. His stiff wrists would hinder the arc and motion of the club head. When he learned to allow his arms to move from the shoulder joint freely without tension, and the wrists to bend to the motion of the club, his body's response to the use of the club was absolutely perfect. No longer did he hit the ground. His shoulder pains disappeared and his game improved.

The second individual had to learn to hold the club correctly and stop the roundhouse type of thought with the club and body. He also learned to keep the body in its original position when allowing the arms to place the club back and to wait for the arms to return to the ball before getting involved further. With the correct grip he was able to coordinate his hand and wrist action to the use of the club, keeping the club face square, and to assist the action with the body toward the hole. His short game improved rapidly and he is no longer shanking the ball.

Whenever the body is subservient to the hands and arms and coordinates to their movement, you can have coordination and synchronization—not mechanical manipulation—at any age. The body should assume a position of ease at address, and remain in this attitude throughout the action. Regardless of your age, you can use whatever strength and flexibility you have to advantage and richly enjoy the delights of golf.

Always use strength, flexibility well

Arthritis

Those with arthritis and bursitis will have difficulty because movement usually causes pain. The fingers cannot close easily and pain results when pressure is placed upon them by the weight of the club or during the swinging motion. The shoulders do not move freely.

Those with finger and wrist problems must learn how to hold the club with merely enough strength to move the weight. The pressure should be comparable to that of holding a bird in the hands. When the weight is placed into motion, it will pull on the fingers and one should increase the pressure sufficiently to maintain control but no more than that.

Increase pressure to maintain control

Move the wrist and forearm as one unit in conjunction with the club head without bending the wrist joint. Do not lever the wrist to develop a snapping position for the club. You will feel as if the hands and forearms are one unit in their action. Never keep the left arm stiff. If it bends when moving the club away from the ball, fine; the right also bends and they both bend again after the ball has been hit.

In one instance, I had an individual place the handle in the right hand with the palm facing upward and the left palm over the handle facing the ground. This is just the opposite of the proper grip. Yet it worked well. You

On learning the proper grip

will feel that you loop the club near the top, but this will be controlled when you begin the return toward the ball in a calm manner.

Don't attempt speed, power or strength in bringing the club against the ball. Your intention should be to allow the weight to fall against the ball and help it continue into the finish. Keep the muscles flexible.

When arthritis is in the shoulder joints, I would not recommend a great deal of motion from the arms. You may have limited motion on the way back, but this should not frustrate you. With help from the body to assist the arms, you can move the club through the ball into the finish. Many times the finish will end low and in front of you.

The body in this instance will be a pushing agent when and only when the club reaches the area where the ball is resting on the tee or ground. This will unite the action of the arms and shoulders so there will not be a separate motion of the arms from the shoulder joints. You can allow the elbows to bend on the way back and keep the upper arms from raising very high at all. Your hands and forearms produce a whipping action against the ball. When the ball has been struck, allow the arms to bend again at the elbow finishing in front of you. This action works very well for those who have arthritic condition of the shoulders.

How body becomes a pushing agent

So learn to take the club back to a point where the pain is not severe. Allow the arms and club to return toward the ball, and use the body to assist in a pushing motion with the arms, hands and club to hit the ball. Be content with the distance you can generate with this action. As you build confidence in your ability to send the ball up in the air and straight, as well as to a certain distance, greater distance will result.

When you have neck difficulties, you also should make a unified motion to the right and to the left. You will feel as if you are in one piece with the shoulders.

216

You may have free use of the arms from the shoulder joints. This will be of great help. The ball can be seen out of the corner of your eyes when you have limited motion of the head. When you calmly move to a point of organization away from the ball but suited to you, and calmly reverse your action, you will be soundly balanced over the ball to strike it sharply.

Soundly balanced, strike the ball

If you have freedom in the fingers and wrist joints, you can use this motion to great advantage. Greater wrist action will create a larger arc for the head of the club to strike the ball sharply. While you may be limited in your physical movement, the head of the club can be used in a larger arc around you. Check out which movement allows the greatest club head work for maximum force against the ball with the least amount of pain. Then concentrate on this.

Back Problem
As one who has suffered with a back problem, I can relate well to those in a similar situation who wish to play golf. My problem began when I fell 300 feet and landed on my back. I still suffer pain if I use a club improperly. If you will learn the easy way to handle the club, you can enjoy a good game in spite of this difficulty. You will come to appreciate golf as much as I do.

Back hurts; use club properly

And I am not alone. Here is what Dr. Paul Ravenna wrote me recently:

"This is remarkable because you started me in active sport after almost 40 years of inactivity—at the age of 68—with a history of severe lumbrosacral backaches, disabling at times, and arthritis of both shoulders, one of which had unsuccessful surgery years ago.

"Following your instructions, at no time did I feel any painful strain in my back or major joints. I was truly surprised that I could do so much without eliciting pain.

"In addition, my wife, age 62, who suffers from cer-

No painful strain
when done right

vical arthritis and radiculitis requiring constant attention to the stance of her head, has been able to improve
her game without at any time feeling any adverse symp-
toms during or after your instruction and this is really
a great achievement for you."

Remember that you must avoid all strain upon the
back from muscle tension during the action of the club.
*You must depend exclusively upon the free use of the
arms from the shoulder joints.* The arms must be
allowed to control the action completely. The body
must receive its signals from them and coordinate with
them throughout the motion.

Right hand above
right shoulder

An easy way to learn how to perform the motion free
from tension is to place your right hand just above your
right shoulder with the wrist bent backward. Move
your right hand to a finished position, face high, well
out in front of you, bending the wrist joint again toward
you. Allow the body to follow the hand into a balanced
position perfectly straight. Perform the same action
with the club in your hands. *Remember, the body
follows the hands.*

At no time should you attempt to shift your weight,
bend over greatly—even in the short irons—or develop
muscular force in an effort to hit the ball greater distances. Of all people, you must depend upon the smashing of the weight at the end of the shaft to pick up centrifugal force and send the ball far and accurately.

The more you react with a flexible, resilient body, the
more synchronized your impact against the ball will be
and the farther you will hit it. In addressing the ball,
you may have to stand more erect than normal. In this
case the wrist may be raised somewhat. Speed is

Speed develops
as hands act

developed as the body serves as center for the action of
the hands. The lie of your clubs may have to be more upright. How extreme or upright your position is will
depend upon the severity of your problem. So the
change in lie of your clubs will also depend upon this

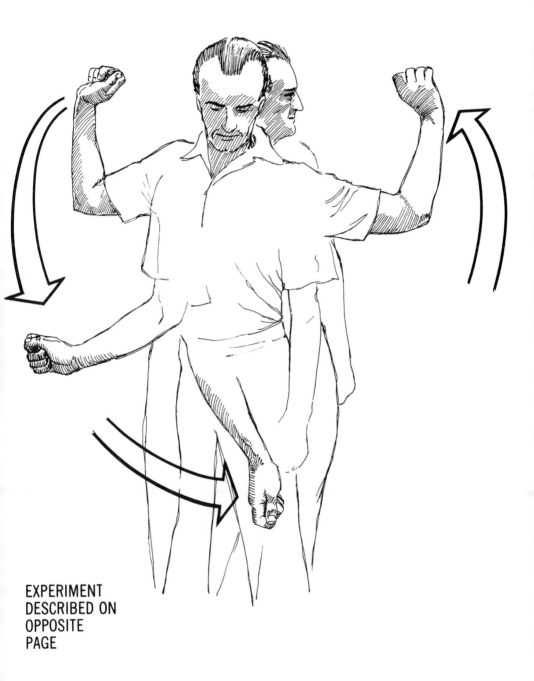

EXPERIMENT
DESCRIBED ON
OPPOSITE
PAGE

condition. If your problem is not severe and you can bend somewhat, maintain the hand and arm relationship at the wrist joint as described in the chapter on balance.

Never place the club back away from the ball too far, for this will cause you to fluctuate off the ball, demanding more body movement than necessary and causing pain. Never use the hips to initiate the action. When you use the hips, they will move in one direction and the upper portion of the body in another direction, causing pain. You can learn to eliminate excessive movement.

Hips should not start action

After years of pain, Andrey Spak was told to give up golf. With the author's instruction she now plays golf pain free in spite of a spinal disease.

Never attempt to develop speed physically. This causes unnecessary hip and leg motion. Coordination cannot be developed when portions of the body (hips, legs and feet) move separately from other portions of the body (hands, arms and shoulders). While in a more upright position, you must develop a unified movement of hips and shoulders, controlled by the hands, arms and club. The entire body turns toward the right slightly and then completely into the finish. This synchronized movement will enhance timing and force against the ball. This can be achieved only through

Mental control aids synchronization

mental control—a control which you can develop.

Short shots will not demand much movement from the body, particularly away from the ball. The body should coordinate with the club head through the ball into the finish regardless of the limited, backward, independent movement of your hands and arms. The closer you get to the green, the less your body is needed. The hands and arms will move more. When the ball is next to the green, the hands do almost all the work. *In all shots, the arms must move freely from the shoulder joints.*

**Right hand
should tap ball**

Putting remains a simple tap of the ball regardless of your body position. The severity of your spinal condition will dictate your position. Whether you stand tall, partially bent over, or bend considerably, the right hand still taps the ball. You can find a suitable centralized position from which to use the putter. Place the ball so the back of the ball is hit easily.

The use of the sand iron should be the same as described in the chapter on sand work. You will need to be very careful with the lies which are downward or upward, buried deep in wet sand, or against the slope of a trap.

Make a strong foundation and allow the arms to move independently from the shoulders. Use the hands to develop the force to make the sand push the ball out and onto the green. You will discover how free action of the arms from the shoulders can develop such force. Always develop centrifugal force with the head of the club.

In all shots an individual with back problems must depend upon the weight of the club to strike the ball. It will feel as if the weight falls against the ball, receiving your help from this point into the finish.

If you have problems in the upper portion of the back, you cannot turn the shoulders easily. You must be satisfied with placing the club back a short way, but maintain free body movement with the club in a full motion into the finish. Remember, it is the club head controlled by the hands which sends the ball prodigious distances accurately.

A man with a fused spinal column has limited mobility of the shoulders also. How can he get his shoulder under his chin, make a full turn, extend the left arm, get the hips out of the way, and pull with the

Fused spine limits mobility

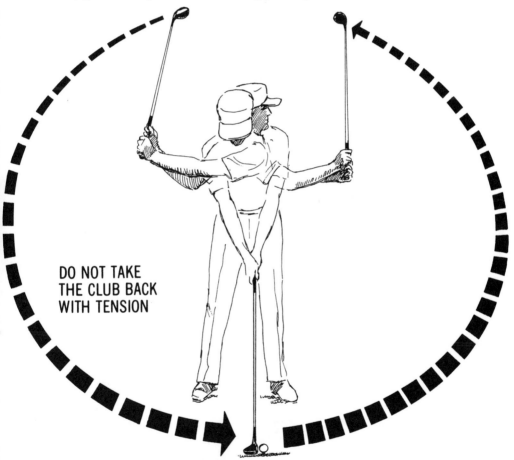

DO NOT TAKE THE CLUB BACK WITH TENSION

IN ALL SHOTS, THE INDIVIDUAL WITH BACK PROBLEMS MUST DEPEND UPON THE WEIGHT OF THE CLUB TO STRIKE THE BALL.

left arm while the shoulders are still back of the hips? It seems impossible.

Use the club the best way you can, but not mechanically like a robot. You are a human being with instincts which will dictate moves you can tolerate and control. Why not give God the benefit of the doubt? He has made you wise enough to understand your situation and adjust the use of the club to that situation.

Some back problems generate pain down the legs. These are among the most difficult to tolerate. However, I have had the pleasure of teaching such individuals to find a position which allows them to strike the ball with limited speed. The surprising thing was that they hit the ball farther than they had anticipated.

Strike ball with limited speed

The weight of the club was allowed to fall against the ball and the arms used to move the club into the finish. This took the strain off the back because force was applied or generated toward the ball upward into the finish. The weight of the club, hands and arms now reached the bottom without strain. Then the arms helped the club upwards into the finish. This actually is the way every golfer should learn to use the club, regardless of his physical condition. Thus the body will be able to respond and move as a unit through the ball into the finish in a well-coordinated action. I recommend this as a practice for all players.

Move as unit through the ball

In this book I have attempted to free everyone who wants to play a good game of golf from the many theories which ask the player to exercise extraordinary physical movements to achieve success. Through personal experience, I have discovered my painless, comfortable golf method. Anyone can benefit from this natural way to play the game. I trust that as you apply the principles outlined in this book, you will not only improve your scores, but you will find golfing to be more fun and more fulfilling.